Fifty Ways to Greater Well Being and Happiness

Robert Pawlicki, Ph.D.

Robert Pawlicki, Ph.D.

ISBN-13: 978-1479218783

ISBN-10: 1479218782

Most folks are about as happy as they make up their minds to be. –

Abraham Lincoln

Dedication

To my marvelous wife, Gail Scarbrough

Fifty Ways to Greater Well Being and Happiness

Preface

"And they lived happily ever after." From our earliest stories we are told that there is a nirvana to be found somewhere; marry the princess, be swept away by the prince, find the pot of gold at the end of the rainbow, hit the Lottery jackpot. Books end with it. Fairy tales promise it. Movies wallow in it. Happiness — we all pursue it, and the drive to find it is endless. Perhaps that's why bookstores seem to be filled with books promising us the secret to finding it. We can dismiss most of these promises as hyperbolic salesmanship, but the reality is that happiness is a never-ending attractive commodity. No matter how many books are in the bookstore, there will continue to be a market for what we all seek — happiness.

In this day and age, the study of happiness has moved beyond poets and philosophers describing it. Psychologists, after ignoring the topic for a century, have rushed in to put their scientific stamp on the topic. Armed with surveys, personal questionnaires, physical measurements and brain scans, they have provided a bevy of new data to accompany the poets and philosophers of the past. We see Blue States compared to Red States, countries repeatedly measured over time, trend lines for men and women and even searches for a happiness gene.

There appears to be an endless appetite for the subject and with good reason. Once we get past basic survival, we humans are built to move beyond simple gratification. Yes, it's true that we are constantly seeking pleasure, but our unique frontal cortex is more than a primitive reward seeker. Our ability to think abstractly, cogitate and ruminate puts us at the top of the evolutionary chain, not merely seeking the next biological satisfaction. Primates may take pleasure in securing their favorite food, but it's hard to imagine one enjoying a delightful memory of childhood, the thrill of an adventure or the enthralling experience of solving a deeply complex problem. No, happiness is more than short-term pleasure. Many scientists have even moved beyond the happy mood state associated with happiness and have proceeded onto a more rigorous term — well being. This designation includes subcategories of positive emotions — engagement, accomplishments, relationships and meaning. But whether we call it happiness or well being, each has much to do with attitude, philosophy, habits and style, customized in a million different ways for billions of different people, and we're all trying to find it.

In our search, many of us would like a little genie sitting on our shoulder giving us guidance, or perhaps a map onto that yellow-brick road. Given the low likelihood of such an occurrence, we continue to read books, articles and columns — I know, I write one. Actually I've been writing one for four years and during the last fifteen years have often taught classes on the subject.

My column has generated a surprising following. I am often stopped in grocery stores and restaurants with "Are you the fellow that writes the happiness column?" More gratifying are the dozen or more people who tell me that they cut out every column so they can paste them in a binder, creating their own book. Some have compared the column to the book, *Don't Sweat the Small Stuff*, as a brief message with a powerful punch.

One of the most fascinating facts about happiness is that

most people have a general idea of what makes them happy — they simply don't practice what they know. We know we are happy being with friends, but we don't spend enough time with them. We know it is important to compliment loved ones abundantly, but it is hard to do when we notice their faults. We know that we sometime don't look at the big picture but get focused on the discomfort in front of us.

Of course, not everyone procrastinates, avoids the work or forgets, but enough do to make a pleasant, easy-to-read reminder a great aid. And to make it all the more powerful, let's make the message so simple and enjoyable that a reader can read the same material time after time.

Made up of two to three page messages, *Fifty Ways to Greater Well Being and Happiness* provides exercises that convert the empirical findings of the new field of Positive Psychology into practical recommendations. The brief suggestions are also like a refreshing alternative to the stresses of the day, providing new goals that encourage hope for tomorrow. Undoubtedly, some will become favorites and read repeatedly to comfort and motivate.

Millions of people have found enjoyment and inspiration in reading self-help books. In my study of happiness, I have read dozens of them and my favorites, not once, but many times. They remind me of personal truths and provide a reminder for behaviors and habits that have carried me, and my clients, through difficult times. For example, when I examine negative emotions, I often find that they are fueled by distorted thoughts such as over-generalizing, losing perspective or discounting the positive. Catching these patterns encourages a person to take control of those things that they can control, thus spurring them to move beyond their sadness. *Fifty Ways to Greater Well Being and Happiness*, is a similar reminder — a very quick one. When kept as a near-by reference, the advice provided in this book can be a valuable tool in maintaining and enhancing a general state of happiness and Well Being.

My wife and I have found reading to each other, especially during long drives, to be a pleasant and bonding experience. Particularly enjoyable have been books that offer brief exercises that prompt us to share ideas and feelings. (John Gottman's book, *The Seven Principles for Making Marriage Work*, is such a book). I suggest that *Fifty Ways to Greater Well Being and Happiness*, and particularly a discussion of the exercises, would offer a similar pleasure.

Of course, good reading (and good advice) is often absorbed at bedtime. When so many people end their day with worrisome thoughts, for me it is the ideal time to replace problems with reminders that happiness is possible. With a little work and a little guidance, the walk onto the yellow-brick road, or at least one not so riddled with potholes, is possible.

Robert Pawlicki, Ph.D.
Savannah, Georgia
September, 2012

Table of Contents

Robert Pawlicki, Ph.D.

Exercises

1

It Is Your Moral Obligation to be Happy

Be good and you will be happy. We've heard that message all our lives, but the sequence is wrong. In fact, we are most good when we are happy. Think about it — when are you kindest? Probably when you are feeling happy. When you are feeling ebullient, you are likely your most "good," generous, charming, and delightful self. And, of course, the reverse is the case as well. When you are unhappy, depressed or miserable, you are self-centered, selfish and probably a curmudgeon, not a pleasant person to be around. Given this perspective, it can be logically argued that you have a moral obligation to be happy, for it is in this state that you will be the most kind to your fellow human beings.

Many people need permission to be happy. They believe they are not worthy, not deserving. They may have been indoctrinated with a childhood guilt that you have to be good before you can be happy. In reality they should have been taught it is important to be happy, and happiness will make it more likely that you will be good, kind and certainly more tolerant.

If we examine those who are very unhappy or depressed, we see the relationship between happiness and goodness even more clearly. Depression is a time of shutting down, turning inward. It is when problems become so dominant that the depressed person is unable to relate to others and has difficulty being compassionate. The person becomes inner focused. It is a time of depleted energy and changes in basic functions such as eating, sleeping, and concentration. Under such circumstances it is difficult for goodness to thrive, for goodness requires energy, compassion and empathy.

Depression, anger and blame narrow our focus. Anger reduces the field of thought and positive behavior. Blame, too, tends to restrict our energy, diverting it away from problem solving, compassion, kindness and creativity. Happiness, on the other hand, widens our scope and this expansiveness opens our world to greater sensitivity, awareness and generosity. Goodness, compassion and empathy are companions to happiness and when expressed, they generate additional rewards of their own.

Making happiness a priority is analogous to the instructions given by the airline personnel that, in an emergency, we place the oxygen mask over our own mouth before we tend to our children. If we place the mask on our child first and pass out from lack of oxygen, we can be of no benefit to our child. Whereas, if we place the mask over our own mouth first, we can revive a child who has momentarily passed out andlater carry him or her to safety. What may initially strike us as selfish turns out to be smart — so too with taking care of our happiness. What appears on the surface to be selfish is, in fact, generous to those we love, for when we are happy we will provide those around us with greater kindness. Therefore, for the sake of others, it is our obligation to work at being happy.

2

Choosing to be Happy

My wife, running, music, ice cream, my dog, kindness — these are the answers people give to the question, "What makes you happy?" The list goes on and on. It is rare for any of us not to have an answer of some sort. The question, "Are you happy?" however, is not so easily answered. People know what makes them happy, but they don't necessarily practice what they know.

Why the inconsistency? The answer may appear obvious. "I can't be happy when I've got to work, take care of my children, or worry about my finances. I'll be happy *after* I get a job, my loved one gets better, I pay off my credit cards." These answers embody the concerns of life that take priority over attention to happiness — even when we know what makes us happy. Understandable, perhaps, but nonetheless curious.

Desiring happiness is universal. Taking constructive action to become happy is not. And yet there are many experts who argue that happiness is a choice. To the distressed, however, there is no choice. Life's pressing problems take precedence.

Take Karen, a 41-year-old married woman, with two teenage boys, and a job as a computer programmer. Between a marriage that's gone stale, boys who create worry and havoc in her home, and her work that she doesn't particularly like, Karen doesn't feel the least bit happy. Karen knows what makes her happy — time with close friends, going to a Yoga class, and reading a good book. But ask Karen if she takes time to engage in these activities and you'll receive a staunch no. There's no time.

A critical question for Karen is this: Are there any other women, her age, in a stale marriage, with two teen boys, working in a job that they don't like, who are happier than she? If the answer is yes, the question then becomes what do these women do that Karen does not?

Fortunately, scientists have observed people who are able to thrive in difficult times. Here are a few of the characteristics that consistently show up: 1) the happier person continues to believe, in spite of difficult circumstances, that she has primary control of her life. Such a belief tends to provide an atmosphere that allows for constructive problem solving as opposed to despair. 2) The happier person arranges at least a small portion of each day to take care of her own needs, even in the face of pressing external demands. It may be as simple as doing a few minutes of exercise, going to a quiet relaxing space or any other activity that is regularly incorporated into her day. 3) The happier person works at maintaining an optimistic attitude, retaining hope and perspective, and seeing the positive aspects within a difficult uation. Being aware of the positive details of life and regularly expressing gratitude for these things is a part of this feature. 4) The happier person uses a support system of friends or relatives to discuss the difficulties of his or her life.

See if you can answer the following questions in the af-affirmative: Do you believe that you are in control of your life? Do you take a small portion of each day to exclusively devote to your needs? Do you maintain an optimistic attitude, even seeing the positive in difficult situations? Do you express gratitude for those things you have? And, perhaps most importantly, do you regularly share your life and concerns with friends and/or relatives?

Notice that all of these things are within a person's control, although all require effort to set in place.

When experts argue that happiness is a choice, they are not suggesting that difficulties disappear. Rather they are saying that we can look at things differently, even in difficult situations. Making sure the above recommendations are in place is a good place to start.

Remember, finding happiness takes effort.

3

Be Kind To Yourself

I often ask classes the simple question "How would you build a child's self-esteem?" Hands immediately go up as if I'm teaching first grade. "Praise them. Tell them how wonderful they are". "Be sensitive," another person blurts out. "Don't criticize all the time, be understanding."

Such is the virtually universal response I've heard time and time again. This voice of compassionate mentoring is laudable, obviously more often done in thought than deed, but praiseworthy. The answer to my next question is not, however, so clear. Do you show the same compassion to yourself? Do you lavish internal praise on yourself and provide sensitive, forgiving understanding of your failures? To this question the hands rarely reach for the sky.

It turns out that treating yourself well is all too uncommon. And it's unfortunate, for what psychologists call "self-compassion," how kindly people judge themselves, is a key to happiness.

Self-compassion (I'm not talking about making excuses) is far better than the alternative many people choose — berating themselves. I often see this on the sports field where players call themselves names they would never dream of using on a child or friend. Not only does such name-calling denigrate the person, it does little to improve performance. Psychologists have long shown that raising the intensity of anger or frustration hinders rather than aids performance.

One of my earliest exposures to popular psychology was a book entitled, "Psychocybernetics" by Maxwell Maltz, a quite influential book in the 1960s. While saddled with many under-researched ideas of the time, his main thesis turns out to have much merit. Maltz argued that we perform most well when we act like a cybernetic machine. He used a rocket as an example. When a rocket is sent toward a distant planet its sensors detect when it's off course and the rocket interprets that information to correct its direction. It doesn't berate, criticize or denigrate its previous erroneous trajectory. When it's on track, the rocket uses positive feedback to maintain its successful travel.

Humans, on the other hand, tend to turn this model on its head. When "off course" they use errors as an opportunity to beat up on themselves. They create static and interfere with the achievement of their goal. They damage their personal self-perception with ill-founded name-calling. Maltz would probably have argued that, if the rocket acted like it's human counterpart with self-criticism, it would probably blow up in flight.

Failures, errors, and missteps are a part of life. How we handle each one influences our ability to manage the next. Compassionately giving ourselves a break not only moves us toward accepting our imperfections but also pushes us away from depression and anxiety and toward optimism and happiness.

It is important to note that self-compassion should not be confused with lowering personal standards. The rocket doesn't change its goal by minimizing criticism; it simply seeks objective data to keep on track. In the human sphere, efforts to increase exercise or lose weight, two of the most common challenges facing Americans, are often derailed when missteps are followed by personal deni-gration. All too often the effort then falls apart. When short-term failures are perceived as a normal part of long-term habit change, the probability of success increases enormously.

Being kind to oneself is a habit worth pursuing. In the course of a lifetime the number of little failures is beyond counting and the opportunity to make self-judgments, compassionate or critical, are endless. The pebbles of criti-cism can build a destructive feeling of inadequacy and a sense of insecurity. Alternately, compassionate responses facilitate a healthy perspective. Self-compassion feeds a stable maturity that in turn nurtures the treatment of oth-ers in a more empathetic manner, wonderful for you and for those around you.

4

Where is Happiness Found?

Many years ago a friend asked if I could chat with her about a problem. She had been widowed for three years after a long marriage and was now ready to begin a new life — but there was no one to begin her life with. My friend began her story by detailing the good, the bad and the ugly from her marriage, focusing mostly on the good, reporting few regrets but now ready to start anew. It was clear that she had done considerable work in moving through the grieving process and was comfortable with her memories.

The problem, as she saw it, was that she could not find a companion, and so there was emptiness in her life. It was not that she hadn't made an effort. Quite the contrary, she had tried singles groups, advertised in magazines and circulated in church settings, but found few opportunities. She was lonely. She wanted to share her life and feel the warmth of a companion.

She was perplexed because she had much to offer. She was a nurse, and artist, worked at her physical fitness, was well spoken and quite engaging. However, in her mind, her life was not complete and would not be until she was a part of a matched pair.

I listened attentively, sympathized with her frustration, but then carefully began to challenge her assumption that her happiness was dependent upon finding a mate. She countered that she knew others who lived happily as singles, but she could not imagine doing so.

Exploring alternatives, she revealed that she had always wanted to travel to Europe, but family obligations had interfered. I gently pushed her to take charge of what she could control and to look inward rather than allowing outside factors to control her happiness. My thoughts are well expressed in a favorite quote by Agnes Repplier, "It is not easy to find happiness in ourselves, and it is not possible to find it elsewhere."

To make a long story short, my friend went to Europe and had a great time, but more importantly she began to change her belief that she could only be complete if she had a partner. An additional factor, a very critical one, is that my friend's vitality, her subtle message, had not been inviting. When she began to control her own life, however, her excitement returned and with it a quantum leap in confidence and attractiveness. Shortly thereafter, she did meet someone and has now been happily married for over ten years.

In her book, "The How of Happiness," Sonja Lyubomirsky notes that, "Happy people are more likely to acquire lovers and friends" and observes that, "Happiness will help you attract more and higher-quality relationships, which will make you even happier, and so on, in a continuous positive feedback loop."

Interestingly, my friend shared my advice with a friend of hers, who then sought my counsel. She, too, had been widowed and was in the same early position, having searched out the "singles scene" and come up empty. Likewise, she had a great deal to offer, but could not find someone to share her life. Our conversation was similar in that I encouraged her to take control of her own happiness by managing her own beliefs and actions. She, too, came to exude a newfound energy, and a relationship soon appeared. Here's where the stories of my two advisees differ. Her new relationship did not last. She did not find a happily ever after story within a relationship. But she did find happiness within herself and continues to be dynamically different than the sad person I saw many years ago.

The true objective was not to find a partner. The real goal was to find happiness, and that can only be done by looking within and controlling what you can, no matter the circumstances. It's not always an easy path to inner happiness, but as Agnes Repplier stated "it is not possible to find it elsewhere."

5

Gratitude Is Worth Much More Than Gold

Jason, Chen, Juan, Kareem, or Alicia — people of every background tend to be happier if they embrace gratitude. Counting your blessings, savoring the positive and becoming sensitive to the good things in your life — even the favorable aspects of negative events — are all forms of gratitude. But, whatever its form, learning to be grateful has boundless benefits. Gratitude, regularly practiced, is highly related to happiness.

Gratitude changes the glasses through which you see the world. It reminds you that positive things are happening in your life. It provides balance when bad experiences, with their ability to dominate, threaten to control your attention. Gratitude, the quality of feeling thankful, allows you to remember and appreciate good experiences long after they are gone. It has also been found to reduce stress and improve health.

Research psychologist Sonja Lyubomirsky has performed

multiple experiments that confirm the link between gratitude and happiness. In one study, participants were
asked to write down five things they were grateful for,
once a week for ten weeks. Another group was asked to
write down five daily hassles or five major events that
happened to them, once a week for ten weeks.

The findings were exciting. Not only did the "gratitude
group" tend to be more optimistic and more satisfied with
their lives, but they also reported "fewer physical symp-
toms (such as headaches, acne, coughing, or nausea) and
more time spent exercising." Other studies with both students and adults have revealed similar results.

How do you make gratitude a habit? Here's a simple
way. At the end of each day write down two things
you're grateful for. List things you appreciate in your life
— your spouse, your children, the beautiful day, etc. A
good trick is to place a paper and pen on your bed each
morning. Do not allow yourself to get into bed at night
until you have completed your daily list.

Writing out your grateful items is critical. The act of writing clarifies and cements them into your mind. Try not to
repeat items. You may be grateful to be married to a wonderful spouse, but it's more beneficial to cite specific qualities. For example, "I'm grateful that my husband likes to
cook" or "I'm grateful that my wife compliments me." By
citing different qualities, you'll find that over time, you'll
become far more aware of what a wonderful spouse you
have.

Researchers have found that for some people daily listing
can lose its punch after awhile, probably because the

words become mere recitation rather than deeply felt. If this happens to you, try doing it two days a week, perhaps Wednesday and Sunday. Be sure you designate the days in advance. Whatever schedule you use, this is a simple but powerful way to increase your happiness.

Robert Pawlicki, Ph.D.

Exercise

Gratitude

Each day, for the next seven days, write down two things for which you are grateful. Do not repeat the items from day to day.

	Things for which I am grateful
Day 1	1.
	2.
Day 2	1.
	2
Day 3	1.
	2.
Day 4	1.
	2.
Day 5	1.
	2.
Day 6	1.
	2.
Day 7	1.
	2.

6

Aging: It's not so bad after all

"Oh my aching back," "Another Senior Moment" — the laments of seniors (remember when we called them "old people"?) Griping about getting old seems to be universal. In many ways it's quite understandable. Our bodies deteriorate, certain movements become painful, energy wanes, friends and family seem to move away or die and, worst of all, the grim reaper moves ever so much closer. Adding insult to injury, our culture celebrates the slimness, firmness, agility, energy, and beauty of youth. With such a picture it's no wonder that we may long for our youth.

But fear not; all is not lost! According to a major study recently published in the American Sociological Review, ". . .as people age, their happiness increases while the differences between genders and ethnic groups narrow." With so many challenges thrown at the aging population, how can that be?

The simple answer is that, for most people, age increases maturity and provides perspective, which, in turn, increases happiness. Of course, not all seniors are happy, but the ones who are seem to have adopted certain perceptions. First, a greater sense of *contentment*. Many of the irritations of the past no longer seem to have great significance. "I have to wait a little longer" or "Everything isn't perfect" is less problematic than at a younger age. Acceptance appears to be a feature of this quality.

Calmness seems to reign more often. Again, the perspective of age tends to diminish the intensity of negative experiences. "I've seen it before," "I lived through it once and I can live through it again" is a more common attitude. Happier seniors seem to know that "this too shall pass."

Another difference, interestingly enough, is in the area of *health perception*. While it is true that pains and physical limitations may increase, happier seniors tend to compare their own distress with those around them who are not faring as well. While seniors may have more health issues, they are well aware of others whose health is far more problematic. That comparison leads them to believe that "I have a lot to be grateful for" — a very significant perspective for happiness.

A fourth area of contrast, between the happier senior and their more youthful counterpart, is the better alignment between aspiration and attainment. In other words the happier seniors are *no longer so distressed by what they haven't achieved,* a common frustration at earlier ages. Age grants perspective, and in many ways we are no longer as critical of ourselves or our achievements as we get older

— a very healthy and more mature state of affairs.

I noted that seniors are happier, on average, than younger folks. It is worth mentioning that those seniors who maintain positive self-perceptions of aging also tend to live longer. In a carefully executed study following 660 subjects for 23 years, researchers found that those with the positive perception lived 7.5 years longer than those with less positive self-perceptions of aging.

So, as with all things related to happiness, our perceptions and focus turn out to be the key to happiness and even to the possibility of a longer life. "Getting old is not for sissies" is a frequent lament, but remember that old age also has gifts for which we should give thanks. It is what we choose to focus upon that is critical to our happiness, even more so as we age.

7

Failure to Forgive: It's not worth it

For many people, a major obstacle to finding happiness is harboring grudges and failing to forgive.

A number of years ago I met a woman whose philandering husband had left her virtually penniless at his untimely death. Although her husband had died two years earlier, she was still seething, unable to get past her anger. Unhappy during most of her marriage, she continued in a state of misery, her husband still controlling her life.

To blame is to lose control. While blame may be understandable, it centers all your energy on the negative. Just as importantly, it places control of your emotions in the hands of the blamed individual, beyond your reach. Nelson Mandela, who was imprisoned for 27 years, was once asked how he was able to bring himself to forgive his jailers. His reply was humanity at its best: "When I walked out of the gate I knew that if I continued to hate these people I was still in prison." Unlike the widow above, he moved on, not controlled by hate or blame.

Some actions are so awful that they cry out for blame. But people who are able to overcome blame avoid narrowing their lives. While blame restricts, forgiveness frees. Where blame interferes with constructive problem solving, forgiveness opens life to new possibilities.

Most people incorrectly believe that forgiveness means accepting the guilty person's actions and absolving them of responsibility. On the contrary, you may still find the actions detestable, but forgiving them allows you to move forward rather than replaying past wrongs. Long term anger and resentment serve only to hurt *you*, both emotionally and physically. Forgiveness is for *you*. It allows you to increase control of your life.

The first step is deciding to forgive. But real forgiveness takes effort. Here is one exercise that experts have found helpful in increasing your readiness to forgive. Write out (and writing is critical) all the circumstances that may have influenced the guilty party's actions. (e.g., He had a miserable childhood himself.)

Another approach is to write down what not forgiving does to you. How has it harmed you already and how may it harm your future?

It may take repeated tries, but remember finding happiness takes effort.

Exercise

Forgiveness

1. State the offending behavior.

2. List (and writing is critical) all the circumstances that may have influenced the guilty party's actions. (e.g., He had a miserable childhood himself.)

     a.

     b.

     c.

3. Write down what not forgiving does to you. How has it harmed you already and how may it harm your future?

     a.

     b.

     c.

8

Acceptance: The path to a calmer life

There are many benefits to accepting those things that we cannot change. In our lifetime, every one of us has a parent, child or friendship that has driven us to distraction or worse. Perhaps it's someone's personal bad habits, bigotry, or opinionated manner. Whatever the source, we all know that certain behaviors can "drive us crazy," if we allow it. It is that last phrase — "if we allow it" — that is key. When we no longer allow it to affect us, but to a large degree accept that it is outside our control, we have moved to a higher level of maturity.

However, acceptance takes considerable effort and mental discipline, perhaps nowhere more so than accepting our own perceived deficiencies. Much of our life involves an inordinate amount of attention to what we perceive as our inadequacies. We may think ourselves too dumb, too short, too tall, too ugly, or fill in the blank with your personal favorite.

Imagine how much energy we would save and how much happier we would be if we added a modicum of acceptance. Even better, imagine if we not only accepted the deficiency but also looked to our strengths to compensate for our weaknesses. Take Edward O. Wilson, Professor at Harvard University, winner of two Pulitzer prizes, and world-renowned naturalist. He writes this of himself:

> "I am blind in one eye and cannot hear high frequency sounds; therefore I am an entomologist. I cannot memorize lines, have trouble visualizing words spelled out to me letter by letter, and am often unable to get digits in the right order while reading and copying numbers. So I contrived ways of expressing ideas that others can recite with quotations and formulas. This compensation is aided by an unusual ability to make comparisons of disparate objects, thus to produce syntheses of previously unconnected information. I write smoothly, in part I believe because my memory is less encumbered by the phrasing and nuances of others. I pushed these strengths and skirted the weaknesses."

How many of us would have become victims or avoiders, filled with self-doubt, given the difficulties encountered by Edward O. Wilson? The trick may be, like Wilson, to spend less time devoted to our deficiencies and far more time attending to our strengths.

Look around in your own life. What are the things that you truly cannot do anything about and would be better off accepting? You might want to write out some self-more constructive alternatives.

Try replacing "I've never been very smart" with "While I may have difficulty with math, I've got a remarkably good memory for details." I'm dumb or not very smart is a global label that doesn't fairly examine the breadth of your intelligence. It's a generalization that only does harm by encouraging self-pity and doubt.

Here's another example: If you blame yourself by thinking, "My son's life is a mess", you may be implicitly thinking "and it's my fault." Such thoughts can be changed to "It's true that my son is having a difficult life. He has also had many bright spots in his life. I did the best I could under the circumstances, and now he has to make his own choices and live with the outcome." This more constructive interpretation would include the acceptance that your son has made his own choices, that many things were outside of your control, and that you are not responsible for your son's actions now. Focusing exclusively on the thought that your son's life is a mess is traveling on a road to frustration and sadness.

Acceptance is quite a challenge. But if we put energy into meeting this challenge the rewards are enormous.

Exercise

Acceptance

1. Draw a line down the middle of a blank sheet of paper.

2. In the left column write down a recurring thought or irritation that you find annoying.

3. In the right column list arguments counter to your annoyances.

4. Consider the following in creating your counter arguments:

   a. Perspective: How important is the annoying behavior to you in the "big picture"?

   b. Harm to yourself: What is the actual harm that the annoying behavior is doing directly to you?

   c. Irritation to others: How might your irritation be affecting people around you?

   d. Under your control or not: What actual control do you have over this annoying behavior? If you have some indirect influence, ask yourself if you are tak- that action. If not, consider accepting the annoying behavior as "part of life."

9

Disability and Happiness: You'll be surprised

What would you say if someone told you that people with disabilities are happier, as a group, than you are? Most likely, you wouldn't believe it. How could that be, with all of the challenges the disabled face? Well it turns out, according to many studies in the new field of Positive Psychology, that people with disabilities tend to be slightly happier than the "able" population.

Don't assume that these findings mean that happiness was easily achieved. Those who become disabled as a result of a trauma typically undergo a substantial period of adjustment during the initial months following their injury. It is after this period that people typically return to their pre-injury emotional state, *Plus*. It is the *Plus* that is fascinating.

The *Plus* includes many who claim to have benefited their experience. That's right, people often claim that their disability was a *positive* turning point in their lives!

They now pause to appreciate things that they formerly took for granted. Others commonly reprioritize their lives, finding that things previously thought to be important have become *insignificant*. This change in their core perspective — a mental paradigm shift — seems to account for increased levels of happiness.

In addition to invigorated feelings of appreciation and a reprioritization of what is important, people with disabilities often find a new sense of purpose. Facing new limitations requires a high level of commitment and willpower. For those previously rudderless, this new direction can replace feelings of emptiness that preceded their disability.

What does this say to those of us who are fortunate enough to be able-bodied? Most obviously, it highlights the importance of examining our priorities and purpose. If we follow the example of those who have "benefited" from their disabling experience, we would learn a daily appreciation of life. We would be reminded that our obsession with many of the irritations in life is misplaced, unimportant in the larger realm of things. And, once again, we would reinforce that our perceptions and focus are the primary key to our happiness.

Some of us are uncomfortable around people less physically able. We might want to rethink those perceptions and realize that maybe we have something to learn from them.

10

Getting Off the Couch Is Good For Your Body AND Your Happiness

Did you know that Nelson Mandela, while imprisoned for 27-years in his matchbox cell, awoke each morning at 4:30 a.m. and did one hour of exercise? Awesome, as some might say.

In difficult times, it is psychologically important to maintain the familiar and control what you can control. Routine is key. In prison Mandela had little freedom and a routine not of his making. Taking charge of what few options he had through daily exercise was one of the ways this extraordinary man maintained his well being as well as his dignity.

The psychological benefits of exercise are apparent when we consider exercise and depression. In my twenty-five years of clinical work, working with thousands of depressed patients, I have never encountered a clinically depressed patient who was also a major exerciser. The two, depression and serious exercise, appear to be incompatible. From a clinical point of view it makes sense. Very depressed people tend to be inactive, unmotivated and lethargic. They are controlled by their issues and more likely to isolate themselves. Serious exercisers, on the other hand, are likely to be active, independent, social, motivated, and energetic. By exercising, the person is taking control of a significant element in his or her life, while the depressed person feels that his circumstances are controlling his life.

Just imagine yourself doing jumping jacks or some other vigorous exercise while calling out how depressed you are. Unlikely — activity and depression are incongruous. Likewise, it's difficult to imagine someone standing still, shoulders slopped and head drooping saying "This is the happiest day of my life." Again, inactivity and happiness tend to be inconsistent.

If you are a regular exerciser, this information should reinforce your continuous effort. If you consider exercise one of your "shoulds", you might want to remember that starting small is possible. It's amusing to hear the old joke that "I think about exercise every day. Then I roll over and go back to sleep". But it's your life and your happiness.

Pictures of exercisers often show young people, but the power of exercise is most evident in the senior population. In one study, sedentary older adults were required to do a very low-intensity program of walking or resistance/flexibility. Participants showed reduced depression and increased confidence. Astonishingly, these gains were maintained for five years!

Exercise, especially when performed routinely, is the ultimate contributor to happiness. That's right. There are now a vast number of surveys and large well-controlled studies that confirm that exercise may be the most effective instant happiness booster of all activities.

Exercise

Daily physical exercise

For the next fourteen days write down at least one exercise performed each day. Begin small and gradually increase or stay small, but do some exercise every day for fourteen days. It could be as little as 10 minutes — you're building a habit.

Day	Exercise performed each day	How long
1		
2		
3		
4		
5		
6		
7		
8		
9		
10		
11		
12		
13		
14		

11

Kindness: Do it for yourself as well as for others

Here's a simple exercise that's guaranteed to increase your happiness — do five spontaneous acts of kindness, *beyond your normal behavior*, for one day, every week. For example, make Mondays your "Kindness Day," a day in which you pay special attention to doing five *additional* acts of kindness. Pay attention to the effect – how you feel for the moment and how you feel about yourself.

You may argue that such an exercise is silly and in your case unnecessary, for certainly you're already a kind person. It turns out that most people believe that they are kind, even though studies show they tend to overestimate the frequency of their kindness. So try the exercise, just in case you're overestimating a bit. And what's the harm if you overdo it, if that were possible?

Did you notice that my recommendation to increase your acts of kindness is not to benefit the world or to save others — it's for you? You've already been told, probably since you were a little kid, to be kind. Undoubtedly your parents and teachers wanted you to grow into a moral and compassionate adult — quite reasonable. But they probably never told you that it would make YOU happier — and it will. It turns out that kindness acts in a multitude of ways to buttress personal happiness.

Imagine how you feel and think following a good deed. Besides that warm fuzzy feeling, you're likely to view yourself kindly — compassionate, sensitive, considerate, might be words that float through your mind. Such feelings and thoughts, when they occur, promote self-confidence, usefulness, even a self-identity. Helping others also highlights your skills, abilities and character — all areas that support positive well being.

The list of benefits goes on. Kindness leads to feelings of self-control, efficacy and accomplishment. And why not? You're the one making the choice, behaving in a manner that you probably know something about and providing benefit to another.

Perhaps the most profound benefits of kindness are the cascade of consequences good deeds engender. Helping people leads others to appreciate and like you. In time, grateful people may reciprocate, providing that network of support that elevates your feeling of security. On the most basic level, acts of kindness cement those connections with others that are critical to your sense of self.

Kindness also takes you away from your problems. Virtually everyone has heard some version of the story of a grieving spouse who throws herself into acts of charity and finds her own grief significantly alleviated. It's hard to feel sorry for yourself when you are connecting with others and feeling compassionate.

No particular talent, ability, amount of time or money is needed for acts of kindness. Nor is it necessary to think up exotic favors; kind words, small deeds, gifts, and services go a long way in bringing a smile to other faces.

You may have heard very generous volunteers say, upon being praised for their effort, that they "gained more than they gave." It's been said, with much truth, "Those who bring sunshine into the lives of others cannot keep it from themselves."

Robert Pawlicki, Ph.D.

Exercise

Kindness

For the next four weeks choose one day per week to per-form four acts of kindness beyond your usual acts of kindness, and record them below.

Acts of kindness performed	
Week 1	1.
	2.
	3.
	4.
Week 2	1.
	2.
	3.
	4.
Week 3	1.
	2.
	3.
	4.
Week 4	1.
	2.
	3.
	4.

12

What Exactly Is A Happy Life?

Most people have a simple picture of happiness: laughter, energy, lack of worry, smiles, and friends. A thoughtful examination of what constitutes happiness, however, reveals that it is much more complicated.

Who of the following would you say led a happy life: Hugh Hefner, Nelson Mandela, Mahatma Gandhi, Martin Luther King, Michael J. Fox? If you could ask them, I suspect all would say they had a happy life — but for entirely different reasons, and few would be citing the picture noted above.

Take Hugh Hefner, the personification of physical pleasure, at least in the minds of many young men during the past 60 years. Whatever the first impression, serious thinkers and scientists studying well being tend to believe that physical pleasure is a most fragile happy state. So, while they might not dispute Hefner's self-perception of happiness, they would argue that a life based on satisfying one's basic needs, in the extreme, is a limited life. They might also suggest that images of frolicking Hefner belie the complications of daily living. Psychologist Martin Seligman notes that the public and even his fellow happiness researchers put too much emphasis on transient pleasures and displeasures. He suggests that momentary measures miss the big picture.

Researchers who look beyond a life spent seeking pleasure might see those who live a "good life" as worthwhile and happy. The experts say those who live a "good life" know their basic personal strengths and live in harmony with those strengths. These are people who find purpose in work, family and avocations consistent with their fundamental character. They are eager to get to work, their avocation or to spend time with family because these experiences are intrinsically satisfying to them. Activities that, from the outside, may appear uncomfortable may be personally satisfying to them. Examples include lengthy scientific fieldwork, caretaking of the underprivileged or proud work as a fireman. The "good life" is self-satisfying and tends to benefit others immediately around the person. We don't have to cite a famous name for this category, just look around and you'll think of someone.

Then there are well-known people such as Nelson Mandela, Mahatma Gandhi and Martin Luther King. Nelson Mandela, who spent 27 years in prison, Mahatma Gandhi, who lived a Spartan life devoid of western pleasures and Martin Luther King, whose life was filled with significant struggles: do they qualify as living happy lives? Actually, according to Martin Seligman, these men lived happy lives of a higher order — a meaningful life. Not only did they live lives of purpose, they expressed character harmonious with their purpose. But, most importantly, they lived lives not just for their own selves, but also for the greater good.

Michael J. Fox is a special case worth noting. In his book, *Lucky Man*, Fox says that, while he was famous and rich, he was actually quite unhappy, addicted and lonely. It was his diagnosis of Parkinson's Disease that redirected his life, gave him a "gift", and lifted him out of addiction and depression. In this one person we see the transformation from an unhappy life, in spite of external appearances to the contrary, to a much happier life, in spite of external appearances to the contrary.

So what is a happy life? Well, it depends how you define it. With thought, we realize that it comes in many forms and styles. Seek pleasure, of course. You're hard wired to do so. But understand that happiness also comes from living a purposeful life, a life in harmony with your personal strengths and one in which your behavior benefits others.

13

Life Is Difficult: It's true

"Life is Difficult." That is the opening line in Scott Peck's book, *The Road Less Traveled*. He goes on to say that once we accept that life is difficult, truly accept it, then life becomes less difficult. But he argues we humans have a strong tendency to personalize our problems as though we were the only ones experiencing such woes.

Unitarian minister Robert Fulghum tells a story that illustrates this propensity. Fulghum writes of a summer when as a young man, he worked at a camp and was miserably frustrated with the boring food, among other things. One day when he was again grousing, he was confronted by an older man who scolded him, "Fulghum, you don't know what a problem is. If you break your neck, if you have nothing to eat, if your house is on fire, then you got a problem. Everything else is an inconvenience."

The scolding man knew. He knew the difference between a problem and an inconvenience. He was a survivor of

Auschwitz. To him any food was a gift. Fulghum was having a pity party — poor me, I have to eat this boring food, life should treat me better. Peck would have said, "Tough," just as the Auschwitz survivor scolded, "Inconvenience — nothing more."

Happiness involves knowing the difference between a problem and an inconvenience. It means being aware that most of life's difficulties are inconveniences, and we're much better off labeling them as such.

If we are honest, we can all admit that we sometimes personalize and magnify our problems. It is not the occasional lapse that is worrisome. It's the philosophical approach of those who routinely adopt this attitude and believe they should not experience the trials and tribulations of life, who are headed for trouble. From such a narcissistic perspective, especially for those truly capable of pity parties, happiness is a distant place.

Woody Allen has written: "Life is full of misery, loneliness, and suffering — and it's all over much too soon." Perhaps much of the misery, loneliness and suffering is part of our own doing, aided by the personalizing that Peck speaks of. How many of these feelings would be lessened if we accepted that "Life is difficult" and moved on? Smiling at Woody Allen's remark acknowledges that, of course, life is difficult and over too soon, but perhaps less difficult if we don't turn the inconveniences into problems.

14

Self-discipline: At the heart of well being

In my life I am guided by the aphorism "The price of freedom is eternal vigilance." This statement is ascribed to Thomas Jefferson and assumedly was meant in a military context, that is, our country can only be free if it is forever on the alert against its enemies. Interestingly, walking around our nation's capital, one sees Jefferson's words engraved on buildings and monuments in many variations but true to his notion — "Freedom Comes From Eternal Vigilance," "Vigilance Is the Cost of Freedom" and so on.

My own exposure to Jefferson's words came from a counselor, not over military matters, but over the value of self-discipline. For the vigilance that Jefferson spoke of requires self-discipline and, just as our country needs to be vigilant to be free, I was told and have come to believe that vigilance in the form of self-discipline leads to personal freedom.

Be it healthy behaviors, attention to showing caring to those we love or the daily ritual of being grateful, those people who exhibit self-discipline are more in charge of their lives and more prone to happiness. Those whose lives are controlled by external circumstances tend to be less happy.

A similar notion, again illustrated by a marvelous quote, is, "There are no short cuts to any place worth going". This thought, from opera singer Beverly Sills, argues that it takes work and self-discipline to attain personal satisfaction.

Self-discipline is a complex topic but here are a few suggestions:

> Examine your internal language. For example, many people are forever telling themselves that they SHOULD diet, exercise, be more assertive — fill in the blank here. Others who do stick to their diet, exercise, etc. say that they MUST diet, exercise, etc. That difference in the internal dialog between SHOULD and MUST is enormous.

> When beginning a new habit, always start so small than you can ensure success. Many failures are based on a fast rewarding start that can't be maintained. For example, do five minutes a day for a week before you increase, rather than 60 minutes the first day and then nothing. The emphasis in building a new habit should be on consistency, not accomplishment — that comes later. New habit structures in the brain are built on repetition, not

spikes of behaviors. Keeping a record of your early compliance is a good way to get a new habit started.

After achieving early compliance, re-label yourself. For example, "I'm a non-smoker," "I'm a healthy eater," "I'm a runner," etc. State your new self-perception in the positive. Even though your habit at this stage may be weak, the re-labeling of your self is cement in the building of your new structure. The more you practice, the more confidence you will have in your new perception, and the stronger your habit will become.

In contrast to appearances, self-discipline is not a burden that restricts but a key to greater freedom. In my own life I have found the discipline and routine of physical fitness provides me energy in other endeavors. The self-discipline of regular gratitude gives me perspective which, in turn, helps stabilize my emotions. The self-discipline of speaking up avoids feeling victimized by circumstance. Like all of us, my self-discipline is far from perfect, but the sign hanging in my office, "The Price of Freedom Is Eternal Vigilance," reminds me that the cost of my personal happiness is self-discipline.

Robert Pawlicki, Ph.D.

Exercise

Self-discipline

1. Write down a behavior that you tend to tell yourself that you "should" do. Write the sentence again changing the word "should" to "must."

2. Perform your new "must" behavior for the next three weeks, beginning with the smallest portion of the behavior that will guarantee success. For example, if daily walking is your objective, begin with the shortest possible walk in order to make it very likely that you will comply. Focus on consistency first before seeking accomplishment. Keep a record of your early compliance in the chart on the next page.

3. After achieving early compliance, re-label yourself. For example, I'm a non-smoker, I'm a healthy eater, I'm a runner, etc. State your new self-perception in the positive. Even though your habit at this stage may be weak, the re-labeling of your self is cement in the building of your new structure. The more you practice, the more confidence you will have in your new perception, and the stronger your habit will become.

New Habit Record

Write out new habit

Day   Check mark if performed

1. ____
2. ____
3. ____
4. ____
5. ____
6. ____
7. ____
8. ____
9. ____
10. ____
11. ____
12. ____
13. ____
14. ____
15. ____
16. ____
17. ____
18. ____
19. ____
20. ____
21. ____

After the first fourteen days, re-label yourself.

I am _____ e.g., I am a runner, I am a social person, etc.

15

A Season of Joy and Sadness

Tis the season to be jolly, arms laden with presents, children laughing, grand meals, clinking glasses, warm reminiscences, uproarious laughter, tra la la — isn't that what the holidays are all about?

The holidays are supposed to be a time of joy, when we share love and harmony, when people are happy, friendly and full of good cheer. But therein lies the problem — "supposed to." We have this image of what the holidays are supposed to be like, nurtured by a lifetime of commercials, movies, and annoying people telling endless stories of holiday ecstasy.

With such well-ingrained perceptions of holiday bliss, we are vulnerable to creating expectations that are nearly impossible to achieve. When our experiences fail to meet these unrealistic images, we feel unhappy. With all the "shoulds" embedded in our heads, ("We *should* be able to get along with that insufferable relative," "We *should* be having a wonderful, loving time," etc.) we are likely to head down the road to "holiday blues".

The primary task in avoiding holiday blues is to change expectations and control what you can control — that ever-present key to reducing most malaise. Take one of the most challenging problems — the difficult relative. Like most recommendations, it is easier said than done. First, lower expectations, expect the worse. Then measure your *own* behavior on dimensions like tolerance, respect, civility, and give yourself credit for accomplishing the impossible. Control what you can control.

Some are saddened by expectations that during the holidays relatives should be together, celebrating in harmony, somehow remedying all hurts from the past — a nice but often unrealistic sentiment. Again, address the part of the issue that is under your control. Perhaps now is the time to write that letter you have been avoiding or to stop procrastinating about that telephone call you have been meaning to make. You may not be able to sit around the fire roasting chestnuts, but you may still be able to connect in some small way. No matter what the response on the other end, you can take some action. Link your feelings to those behaviors that you control. The holidays are good excuse to get it done.

While the holidays may not be for everyone, there are ways to avoid the "humbug" scene. You've lived through the holidays before and you will again. No sense in being miserable in the meantime.

16

Optimism Is Not Only Wise, It's Healthy

Optimists are people who see the glass half-full, not half-empty. They are the ones who pick out the positive in an otherwise negative situation — The ones who are more likely to look at the promise of tomorrow than the misery of today. And when they examine the challenges of the day, they tend to see some silver lining in an otherwise dark cloud. Commentator Matthew Henry had the vision of an optimist when, after being robbed, he wrote in his diary:

> "Let me be thankful. First, because I was never robbed before. Second, although they took my wallet, they did not take my life. Third, although they took my all, it was not much. Fourth, because it was I who was robbed, not I who robbed."

If you notice an element of gratefulness in Matthew Henry's writing, a pillar in the makeup of happiness, you are right. That's the sign of an optimist. Optimists tend to be both sensitive to the positive *and* grateful, denying the negative from becoming overwhelming. Also notice the awareness of the greater picture — "it was not I who robbed". This is a positive nuance many of us would have missed.

But it's not just a positive reframing of life's experiences, it's an expectation that life will turn out well. It is this perception that leads to greater motivation, vigor and initiative. This greater sense that the person can direct much of his or her own future is another pillar of happiness.

There's an added bonus to this philosophical style — optimists live longer. If we define optimism broadly to include positive self-perception and positive perspective, we find abundant scientific evidence correlating optimism and longevity. In an eight-year study of 97,253 women, age 50 and over, conducted at the University of Pittsburgh ". . . women who were most cheery were 30 percent less likely to die of heart disease and 14 percent less likely than their pessimistic peers to die from all causes during the study period." Other research focusing upon older individuals found that seniors with more positive self-perceptions of aging (measured up to 23 years earlier) lived 7.5 years longer than those with less positive self-perceptions of aging. These are just two examples of a wide range of research showing those with more optimistic outlooks live longer.

To understand why optimists live longer, it is valuable to examine those behaviors that co-exist with their positive outlook. Research shows that optimists are more likely to persevere and engage in the face of difficulty. Optimism prompts us to engage in active and effective coping.

Whereas pessimism tends to cloud problem solving, optimism tends to nurture it. Optimists tend to make plans and take direct action when facing adversity, have greater social networks, have stronger social relationships and cope better with chronic stress — all factors that contribute to a healthier and longer life.

All of these fine words on optimism sound great, but what do you do if you're not naturally optimistic? It turns out that research also shows that those less optimistic can increase their optimism. One of the most direct approaches is to incorporate a series of valuable questions into your thinking during moments of stress. These questions can break down some of the negative thinking that's frequent during difficult times. Questions like: Have I survived similar situations before? What are the positives in this situation? What lessons can I learn from this event? What personal strengths do I bring to this difficulty? If you write out your stressful situation, then respond to questions that search for the positive and write those answers as well, you can begin cultivating optimism.

Good luck. If you ask me, it's not the meek who shall inherit the world, it's the optimists.

Robert Pawlicki, Ph.D.

Exercise

Optimism

List two personal issues about which you feel a sense of pessimism.

1.

2.

Address the issues by answering the following questions:

Issue number 1

    a. What are the positives in this situation?

    b. What lessons can I learn from this situation?

    c. What personal strengths do I bring to this difficulty?

    d. How can I look at this situation in a specific, objective and balanced manner?

Issue number 2

    a. What are the positives in this situation?

    b. What lessons can I learn from this event?

    c. What personal strengths do I bring to this difficulty?

    d. How can I look at this situation in a specific, objective and balanced manner?

17

"I Can't Help Comparing Myself to Others"

Our culture brainwashes us to outward standards of beauty that are unattainable for all but a small number of genetically gifted people and, even then, usually for a very limited period of time. Pressures for women to have beautiful glowing skin, lustrous shining hair, perfect teeth and a slim yet voluptuous figure, and for men to have a tall, taut, muscular body are the norm, endlessly endorsed as the appropriate standard. Over a lifetime, the overt and covert message that each of us is less than this standard can be terribly damaging and deflating.

Comparing ourselves with others seems inherently human — but utterly disastrous. For our tendency is to cherry pick the best qualities, the most desirous features and the most idealized lives of others as contrast. Such over-simplification leaves us with the feeling that we are less than, inadequate or a failure. It can make us feel as if our demons are unique, certainly not shared by the people with whom we compare ourselves.

Robert Pawlicki, Ph.D.

In reality there are very few, if any, people who are exempt from major calamities and inner demons. The truth is that virtually every life has, at some time, significant problems, fears, and anxieties. No matter how many vacations, fantastic jobs, achieving children and delightful relatives you hear about, don't diminish yourself by believing that other lives are ideal and yours is less.

The tendency to compare ourselves with others is often accompanied by another damaging behavior — hiding our inner self. By doing so we foster the image that our lives are without pain or struggle and even encourage the impression that we are continually happy. Casually sharing our inner fears and demons obviously doesn't make sense, but locking them up is dangerous as well.

Two problems arise from the good front and stiff upper lip behavior. First, we create an unrealistic picture for others that everyone and everything is hunky-dory. Secondly, such protection against weakness, vulnerability or failings leaves us isolated, living a secret life and less likely to intimately connect with others.

Even worse, when everyone is saying "Fine, good, wonderful, couldn't be better" where exactly does that leave us? And then to hear from friends that their vacation, children, grandchildren are so spectacularly grand can be a little disheartening, if not downright frustrating — all a set-up for personal comparison.

It's a mistake to assume that other people are happy and you are not, unless you know them intimately. Personally, the only people I believe are happy all the time are people I don't truly know. Once I know them well, I realize what I observed on the surface is only a part of the picture. I have come to realize that public lives and private lives are usually quite different, a thought only magnified by my years as a therapist.

While comparing yourself with others is a recipe for disaster, sharing your life in detail with your close friends is the pathway to well being. It is in that good listening, caring and mutual sharing atmosphere that a pillar of happiness is built.

Eleanor Roosevelt had it right when she said, "Nobody can make you feel inferior without your consent." I would add "and make you unhappy without your consent."

18

Identifying Your Personal Strengths Is Incredibly Important

For all of our shortcomings, humans can be astounding. I often encounter very bright, sometimes brilliant, people. Their intellectual abilities can be dazzling, their interests varied — government, politics, economics, law, medicine, photography, computer science – you name it, the list seems endless. And it's not just the technical sounding knowledge that impresses me. People with mechanical, carpentry and plumbing abilities can leave me in awe. Then there are personal characteristics. How about those friends who, in spite of long-term pain or illness, maintain an upbeat attitude? Or those who give endless hours helping others? And people with a great sense of humor or a sensitive caring relative who know how to really express love?

To be impressed with others is marvelous. It represents an appreciation of how fortunate we are to be surrounded by such riches. But we must be careful not to be intimidated, for intimidation has a dark side. It implies that we don't measure up. It provides fertile ground for seeds of inadequacies. My mother was one such example. She was very capable herself but could only see the worth of others. With only an 8th grade education, my mother lived her life afraid to venture into the world, fearful to go where she could be measured. The result was many lost pleasures. Too much of her life was spent anxious over potential failure or ruminating over a possible mistake already made — unhappy and unnecessary musings. Part of her difficulty was that she didn't really appreciate the gifts she had. Her life could have been fuller if she had truly taken stock of her many skills and wonderful personal qualities. All efforts to persuade her of these abilities were lost because her fears were deeply embedded and her ability to accept her strengths was weak. Please don't make that mistake.

For many years I made it a practice to ask patients to specifically detail their personal strengths. Most of the time they would fumble, often staring at the floor, uncertain as how to answer. When I prompted them with questions, they would almost always answer in the affirmative. you honest?" "Oh, of course!" "Kind?" "I try to be." Good answers perhaps, but not as strong as they would be with a thorough self-knowledge of personal strengths.

Knowing your personal strengths is a valuable commodity. Such knowledge gives you guidance during difficult times. Take the simple example of a teenager who firmly believes that honesty is one of her virtues. When pressured by peers to shoplift, she is more likely to resist such actions than a similar teenager with no such belief.

Fortunately, the field of Positive Psychology has a marvelous resource to connect you with some of your personal strengths. Go to www.authentichappiness.org and scroll down to "VIA Survey of Character Strengths" and you'll find a questionnaire that has been filled out by thousands of individuals. Complete the survey and you'll gain insight into your positive characteristics. If you persuade a friend or loved one to also fill out the survey, you then, in a delightful exchange, can discuss and share your findings. In the last analysis you'll be getting a picture of your personal strengths and in doing so making them a clearer resource to be used when needed. I strongly recommend that you write them down and keep them available as a reminder of your individual combination of strengths.

It's wonderful to value other peoples' talents and abilities, but it is also so very important for your own well being to appreciate your own.

Robert Pawlicki, Ph.D.

Exercise

Character Strengths

Go to www.authentichappiness.org and scroll down to "VIA Survey of Character Strengths" on the home page. Click on to the VIA Survey of Character Strengths and follow the instructions to complete the survey. After completing the survey, list your top five character strengths below:

1.

2.

3.

4.

5.

During the next seven days record below any behavioral expression of your top five character strengths. For example, I went out of my way to help Janet — kindness.

Day	Behavioral Expression of Character Strengths
1	
2	
3	
4	
5	
6	
7	

19

Fidelity To A Worthy Purpose

Some dear friends recently send me a most gratifying and simple card that said, "Some people make the world a better place just by being in it. You're one of those people." Warm, fuzzy, and mushy perhaps, but it touched a resonant cord. For I want, like most people, to make a dif-difference.

Interestingly enough, when you feel that you have a purpose, feel that you have made a contribution — be it ever so small — it is a major contributor to happiness. The idea is embedded in a famous Helen Keller quote: "Many people have a wrong idea of what constitutes true happiness. It is not attained through self-gratification, but through fidelity to a worthy purpose."

Perhaps one of the most highly cited but dramatic illustrations of how purpose can surmount the most challenging conditions comes from the life and writings of Victor Frankl. Frankl was a Jewish psychiatrist imprisoned in

Auschwitz for three years, experiencing the unimaginable. With over 8,000 deaths in concentration camps every day, with the chance of survival roughly 1 in 28, with unspeakable horrors occurring daily, Frankl was asked to speak to his fellow prisoners during one of the darkest days. He spoke of the most trivial of comforts, quoted Nietzsche ("That which does not kill me, makes me stronger"), spoke of the future, mentioned the past with all of its joys and finally spoke of "our sacrifice, which meaning in every case." Here he is, in a hell most of us cannot imagine, and he speaks of hope. It is his recognition that his captors can take away every visible substance, but they do not control and cannot take away his dignity or his sense of meaning in life.

Frankl was fond of quoting Nietzche's "He who has a why to live can bear with almost any how." When alone in the concentration camp all goals of life were taken away. What remained was the last of human freedoms — the ability to choose one's attitude.

If you read twenty self-help books with a chapter on purpose, virtually every one would reference Frankl. Understandable given its powerful imagery. Our lives, however, likely lack this drama. Nevertheless, the force of purpose remains the same. Purpose grounds us to a heart-felt motive. It focuses our vision and it typically gives us a direction — all elements that provide a sense of well being. For many, however, purpose is difficult to define, a distant removal from the setting of Victor Frankl.

An answer to this problem is to reduce the expectation that every worthy purpose has to be earth shattering. Its magnitude is not as important as its dignity and meaning to you. Caring for another or being a good citizen, a kind person, an excellent artist are all worthy commitments. Committing to any purpose that you decide is worthwhile is in itself all that is needed.

The next step is to define and measure what it takes to reach your purpose. What does it take to be a good citizen? Writing to legislators, newspapers, speaking out on issues? What does it mean to be caring? Volunteer activity? Kind behavior? How often? Once you provide yourself with a stated purpose and begin to act upon your purpose, it becomes time to begin labeling yourself as a person with a purpose (e.g., I'm a caring person, a kind person, an excellent artist).

Think, for a moment, how you would feel as a person who is actively pursuing a defined purpose and behaving accordingly. It is likely that such "fidelity to a worthy purpose" is a mighty fine place to be.

Exercise

Purpose

Every worthy purpose doesn't have to be earth shattering. Its magnitude is not as important as its dignity and meaning to you. Caring for another or being a good citizen, a kind person, an excellent artist, are all worthy commitments.

1. If you are unsure about deciding on a purpose, a good place to begin is to examine your character strengths. Complete the exercise on character strengths if you have not already done so. A commitment to a purpose that is in harmony with your character strengths has a much higher likelihood of success. List two possible life purposes.

1.

2.

2. The next step is to define and measure what it takes to reach your purpose. The more precise and detailed the bet-better. Writing it out is important. Like an outline to a term paper or a report, the specifics will give you a map to follow. Write out a definition and measurements of that purpose on a separate paper.

3. Re-label yourself. Begin thinking of yourself as the person who is achieving his or her purpose. (e.g., I am a civic-minded person; I am an artist; I am a caring person, etc.) Mahatma Gandhi's well known statement is appropriate here: *"You must be the change you wish to see in the world."* Write your new label here:

I am:_____

20

Invest In Friendships: The best safety net you can have

Most of us have given at least fleeting attention to our financial security, knowing that it is wise to invest early for potential challenges later. We would do well to adopt that same philosophy for friendship. Friendship is one of those things that you can never have too much of, and its value only increases with age. It is not surprising then that those with more and deeper friendships appear significantly happier than those without friendship. Indeed, for many, the greatest fear is to end their lives alone.

It is obvious, then, that it is important to nurture and cultivate friendships. But like the admonition to save for retirement, the suggestion to build friendships is often left to a later day. As in the financial analogy, acting now is inconvenient; it involves work and maybe even pain. The work of getting out of a regular routine, taking time and enduring social niceties, the pain of tolerating differences in style and opinion — are the little barriers that make finding and building friendships hard.

Robert Pawlicki, Ph.D.

Finding a friend with whom you truly resonate is difficult. The heart of friendship is trust; trust that the person will be there for you during moments of stress, trust that the friend will really listen to your needs, trust that the friend cares about you so much that he or she will temporarily sacrifice his or her needs if you are in need. Of course, there are other benefits of friendship as well — the ability to be openly frank, to laugh together and to share memories.

For some, these special friendships have just happened, a miracle of happenstance. But for most they have to develop over time. And for virtually everyone, there has been an element of work. It is the work that many avoid, the work of getting out there and making yourself available and then sticking with friends through the normal ups and downs of closeness.

Perhaps the most challenging aspect of gaining and nurturing a deep friendship is that such a relationship requires a degree of vulnerability. For a true friend knows all about you, including your faults, and still likes you. This is where men are at a disadvantage, because they are acculturated to be competitive, particularly with other men. Competition and vulnerability are polar opposites. The result is that men in general have fewer and less intense friendships than women.

Another problem is that men tend to place all of their friendship eggs in one basket, typically their wives. When tragedy strikes and the one friend is lost, the man is devastated and in a much deeper hole than those with many friends. In my opinion, this is a major contributor to the fact that men live an average of 5.2 years fewer than women.

All this is to emphasize once again the value of friendship and that gaining close friendship requires patience, perseverance, effort and work. People don't set about gathering friends to protect themselves against difficult times the way that people save money for challenging financial periods. That sounds too Machiavellian. We want friends for more lofty motives. But the two motives, future support and present enjoyment, can intertwine. Remember, friendship is mutually beneficial. When you seek out others for their friendship and long-term support, you're of-offering the same in return — a very good trade.

The ingredients for close friendship are quite clear — sharing time, listening, caring, being responsible, trust built through availability and reliability. Another ingredient is simply expressing a sincere interest in your friend's life. These are investments that pay the greatest dividends. They are investments in your long-term well being as well.

21

Pain Is Inevitable, Suffering Is Optional

Most of my professional life as a health psychologist has been spent in the treatment of chronic pain patients. Chronic pain, as a diagnosis, refers to the condition of virtually daily, if not omnipresent, pain. It is a hard concept to grasp. Imagine having a constant toothache — and, for many of the patients I saw, a toothache would be a reduction in their pain — everyday.

If that wasn't bad enough, the patients that my team treated had a condition called *chronic pain syndrome,* which means that the pain condition had evolved into affecting the person physically, behaviorally and psychologically. Our typical chronic pain syndrome patients were addicted to narcotic medication, had greatly reduced activity and were depressed. To say that these patients were not happy would be a massive understatement.

You might respond, "Of course they were unhappy. Anyone would be if they were in pain everyday." And you would be mostly right. But our job was to make them happier. That's right. Not necessarily happy but happier. "How in the world could you do that?" — you would probably ask. And then reflectively you might say, "Oh, you would reduce their pain, and that would make them happier." Well, actually we would *not* promise to reduce their pain, because chronic pain is different from acute pain, like a cut or a broken leg, where the body heals and pain ends. If it were *acute* pain, the physician and/or time would help the pain go away. If it is *chronic* pain, then by definition, the doctors and time have NOT been able to help the pain go away. Since we were dealing with chronic pain, we did not promise to eliminate the pain. So what did we do?

The short answer is that we helped the patient manage his or her life, be more active, regain a sense of purpose and overcome addictions and depression in spite of their pain. An extremely difficult but still possible task.

So what does chronic pain have to do with people who are fortunate enough not to have chronic pain? Primarily in the lessons that can be learned.

Life involves pain, physical and emotional, a point that is utterly obvious. Some of life's pain can be resolved, but there are other pains that cannot, and for those with chronic pain, a different approach is required. It involves an axiom upon which our clinic was based: "Pain is inevitable, suffering is optional." This little truth is a pathway to managing extraordinary difficulties in life. "Pain is inevitable" requires acceptance — an acknowledgement that there are some annoyances (a dysfunctional child, a bigoted relative, etc.) that are very unlikely to change and to some degree must be accepted. "Suffering is optional" means that you must focus on those things in your life that you can control and manage them. It means taking responsibility for your own misery and happiness, even when it is incredibly difficult. It was from this premise that we, in our clinic, frequently achieved the impossible, but only, only, if the patient accepted the premise that pain is inevitable, suffering is optional. This is a useful philosophy not just for those with chronic physical pain but for all of us.

22

Acceptance and Perspective, Not Perfection

I imagine that Mahatma Gandhi was a bear to live with. Oh sure, there is that role he played in gaining India's independence, but I'm talking about his day-to-day life. The routine salt enema he gave himself for forty straight years. And weaving may be interesting for a while but, personally, done everyday I doubt that it would wear well (no pun intended).

I've always been fascinated by the details of the lives of great men and women of history. Part of my intrigue is that I assume the grand stories tend to leave out the foibles of our admired brothers and sisters. And that's the part, to me, that makes them human, their flaws woven into their fabric of greatness. Indeed, I'd like to read a book entitled "The Defects of Great Men and Women" — a book that would make these people real.

What does this have to do with happiness? A great deal if you consider that perspective and acceptance are valuable assets in dealing with personal issues. If we were to realize that the most astounding humans, those humans who have accomplished unbelievable feats, are as flawed as we are, then we can be a little more accepting of our own deficiencies. One of my favorite stories along these lines concerns John Quincy Adams. In his mid-life John Quincy Adams wrote in his diary:

> "I am forty-five years old. Two-thirds of a long life have passed, and I have done nothing to distinguish it by usefulness to my country and to mankind."

This is a man who at the time of this writing had held the following offices: Minister to the Hague, Emissary to England, Minister to Prussia, State Senator, United States Senator, Minister to Russia, Head of the American Mission to negotiate peace with England, Minister to England, Secretary of State, member of the House of Representatives and President of the United States. Close to his death at age eighty, John Quincy Adams wrote somberly in his diary:

> "My whole life has been a succession of disappointments. I can scarcely recollect a single instance of success in anything I have ever undertook."

John Quincy Adams is a prime example of how our internal perceptions are the real agents behind our feelings. If his extraordinary achievements can't create a sense of success, then it's hard to imagine what could. But, of course, the lesson is, once again, that it is not the events of the world that create our feelings, it is our interpretation of the events. Given the filter that John Quincy Adams brought to the table, apparently no accomplishment brought him lasting satisfaction.

Be it Mother Teresa, Nelson Mandela, Harry Truman, Ronald Reagan, Abraham Lincoln, Eleanor Roosevelt, or the Dali Lama, a close examination of each life reveals deficiencies.

John Quincy Adams wrestled with depression. It is no wonder. If one's personal happiness is built on external accomplishments and a standard so high as to court ridicule, it is likely to be fragile. Better that we look to our strengths, accept our imperfections, and understand that even the best of humanity is peppered with flaws. Better not to follow the mental filter of John Quincy Adams. It is often hard to be forgiving when we look critically at our own failings. It is even harder to be accepting. But these qualities are important in maintaining a sense of well being.

23

Beliefs: The power to do good or harm

A man who was treated in the clinic where I worked literally took ten minutes to walk across a room. It turns out that his difficulty was a belief that "if I move too fast my spine will crumble." Our team was very successful in altering his condition — so much so, that in three weeks he was walking ten miles a day as measured by a pedometer! How did we do that? We performed what I call a "belief-ectomy," that is we removed his belief.

Our own beliefs, often reflected in our general philoso- of life, are very powerful. They can cause great good or harm.

Strangely, most of us have a difficult time articulating this driving force in our lives. Our basic beliefs have often been relegated to the back of our minds, subject to a difficult, searching recall. It's understandable. The issues and pressures of daily life take precedence.

But beliefs are fundamental building blocks of our identity. They play a critical role in determining the direction of our life. Take one patient I saw many years ago who adamantly claimed that "He who dies with the most toys wins." Still another believed "I can't fail in my father's eyes." Then there are others, like a friend who believes "My life would be lost if I didn't volunteer." You can easily see how each belief, passionately held, could significantly influence the direction and well being of a person.

There are some belief categories that are especially egregious to mental well being: beliefs that harbor blame: "My misery is a result of" – fill in the blank here); others that teem with prejudice ("The poor, rich, minority group is the cause of all of our troubles; the government, big business is going to be the death of us all."); beliefs that view the world in black and white ("You're either my friend or my enemy."); beliefs that look at the world as highly threatening ("You never know when someone is going deceive you."); or cynical ("People are basically untrustworthy").

On the other hand, when beliefs have a positive tone, they are much more likely to reside in a happier and more secure individual. Examples abound: tones of generosity ("In spite of their flaws, people are basically decent."); optimism ("I continue to believe that I will land on my feet."); perspective ("I've been through all kinds of adversity. I'll have more good fortune in the future. I can handle it."); and complexity ("Even people I don't agree with can be good and fair-minded.")

Beliefs can be incredibly stubborn. There is a story told by Abraham Maslow that illustrates the point. According to

Maslow, a psychiatrist was treating a patient who believed that he was a corpse. In spite of the psychiatrist's best logic and effort, the patient continued with his bizarre perception. In desperation the psychiatrist asked the patient, "Do corpses bleed?" "That's absurd," replied the patient, "Corpses do not bleed." After getting the patient's permission, the psychiatrist proceeded to prick the man's finger with a pin, producing a drop of blood. Staring at the blood for a moment, the patient turned to the psychiatrist and exclaimed, "I'll be damned. Corpses do bleed!" This resistance to reality is common.

Although the psychiatrist was unsuccessful in persuading the patient, he was on the right track. Introducing doubt can change beliefs, and doubt comes from an examination of alternative thoughts. In the case of the clinic patient mentioned earlier, the removal of his old belief occurred because we slowly but safety demonstrated that movement was not going to cause his spine to crumble.

When we realize that some of our personal beliefs are harmful to our well being we can take action to change the situation. Obviously, as a retired psychologist, I believe seeking the assistance of an outside professional is a valuable option. But openness with friends and loved ones is another alternative. The critical element is a willingness to consider opposing evidence, always a challenge. In light of just how important beliefs are to our well being, it certainly seems worth the effort.

24

Establish An Emotional Bank Account

British General Monty Montgomery, of World War II fame, is reputed to have told his new wife, "I love you. There, I've said it and I don't ever want to discuss the matter again." And by all reports he never did.

A good story, perhaps, enhancing the image of a rugged military figure. Whether the story is true I do not know, but it flies in the face of what constitutes a good relationship. In my own clinical experience, I find that a spouse who rarely provides compliments, compassion and caring words inhabits a home high in tension. Indeed one of the fundamentals of any good relationship, marriage or otherwise, is what psychologists call maintaining a healthy emotional bank account. Put simply, good relationships rest upon trust and security, and these, in turn, are nurtured by an ample amount of supportive, loving statements regularly placed in the "bank account." It is this behavior that protects the relationship against the inevitable "withdrawals," the frictions that naturally occur in any relationship.

Biologically, we humans are programmed to be more sensitive to negatives than positives — and it's a good thing we are. Our survival is based on finding rewarding experiences — food, shelter, etc. If we miss one rewarding opportunity, we can continue our quest for another. However, we are alert to even one negative or danger — a saber-toothed tiger, a critical boss or a grouchy spouse — for every negative could be life threatening. While we don't face many saber-toothed tigers or similar dangers, we are, nevertheless, hard-wired to be very sensitive to major and minor insults. The consequence of this evolved state is what is called "negativity bias," the principle that *bad is stronger than good*. Our responses to threats are faster, stronger and harder to resist than responses to pleasures and opportunities.

Indeed, according to psychological research on marriages, it takes at least five good or constructive acts to offset the damage created by one destructive act. This power of an insult or offense (a bank withdrawal) makes it all the more mandatory to offset the damage with an avalanche of positives (bank deposits), making sure the bank account has ample resources.

Interestingly, this straightforward idea is a challenge for many. Some have never been in the habit of giving compliments. Others, like General Montgomery, believe it is unnecessary, and still others are somewhat insensitive to the needs of their loved ones. And probably most often, a large percentage believe, *inaccurately*, that they already give an abundance of compliments. (Hint: it is virtually impossible to give too many sincere compliments.) A simple little technique in my practice remedies these deficiencies in most people. It is the "homework" of giving and recording a minimum of five compliments every day to your loved one, a difficult task for many. Even more challenging is the requirement that this *minimum standard* of five compliments a day be practiced for three weeks in a row — a period that typically consolidates a new habit (with refreshers required, especially during stressful times). For those who do their "homework", the results are marvelous.

It's incredible that such a little behavior as regularly giving compliments to someone we love can be as challenging as it is. It's even more surprising in light of the fact that our own happiness is dependent upon strong relationships with loved ones and friends. But it is ever so valuable to pay attention to those behaviors that feed our relationships — which regular compliments do. My recommendation: set up your own bank account today, and be sure you make frequent deposits.

Exercise

Building An Emotional Bank Account

For the next seven days write down three compliments each day. Record only those that are sincerely given.

Day	Compliments given to a loved one each day
1	1.
	2.
	3.
2	1.
	2.
	3.
3	1.
	2.
	3.
4	1.
	2.
	3.
5	1.
	2.
	3.
6	1.
	2.
	3.
7	1.
	2.
	3.

25

Seeking "Flow" As A Personal Goal

My son-in-law is a computer genius. Of course, I could be biased, but the evidence is strong. Not only does he perform the magic that we novices of the world admire, but he presents papers around the country detailing his latest open source software innovations. He speaks a language that most of us don't understand and reads books that we wouldn't touch. Most of all, he lives and breathes the stuff, awakening in the middle of night to note his latest creative idea. And he's as happy as a jaybird.

His happiness is not the kind of happiness that most people think of. Most of us think of pleasure as delight or joy that is more biological and sensory related. But happiness based solely upon biological pleasure is ephemeral and fragile. Pleasures, like the first bite of a marvelous food, the first smell of an incredibly aromatic flower or the comfort of one's favorite music, are wonderful. But each, in turn, is subject to habituation, that tendency of a sensation to diminish with repetition. Our neurons are built to react slower and differently with each occurrence of the same event. It's probably good that they do. We have enough problems with over consuming our pleasures (think of your favorite dessert) without having to deal with every occurrence at maximum impact.

And this is where my son-in-law comes back into the conversation. His life is permeated by what psychologists call "flow." Flow requires a challenging task and a commensurate skill, concentration, clear goals, immediate feedback, and a sense of control. Most of all it requires that time stops – a perfect description of what happens to my son-in-law when he is engrossed in his work. But, of course, it doesn't feel like work to him. It's a form of happiness — flow. It differs from pleasure in the sense that there are no hormonal changes, no heightened emotions (except in retrospect), and no ecstasy — instead a sense that the experience was positive and a wish to return to it again.

The psychologist who has written most extensively about this state of flow is Mike Csikszentimihalyi (pronounced "cheeks sent me high".) Csikszentimihalyi says that flow is a frequent experience for some people but rare for others. In a fascinating experiment, teenagers were given pagers and randomly beeped in the course of day and asked what they were thinking, doing and how engaged they were. Csikszentimihalyi then tracked high and low frequency flow teenagers. The high flow teenagers had hobbies, were engaged in sports and did their homework, while the low flow subjects were "mall" kids, youngsters who spent a great deal of time at the mall. Some would say high pleasure seekers. The differences between the two groups were strong: the high flow teenagers exceeded the low flow teenagers on every psychological measure including self-esteem and engagement — with one exception. The high flow teenagers believed that the low flow teenagers were having more fun, and they wished they could spend more time at the mall. In spite of perceptions of missing out, the high flow teenagers were more likely to make it to college, have deeper social lives and be more successful in later life. Csikszentimihalyi suggests that flow builds psychological capital that can serve a person well later on in life.

Here too, Csikszentimihalyi's findings mirror those of my son-in-law. He, too, felt out of the mainstream as a kid but is now in his stride. And he's not the only one. Flow abounds in people who love to problem-solve, work with their hands, garden, and throw themselves into a book or cooking. It turns out that flow is most often associated with personal strengths and doing things that we love to actively do. The word "active" is critical. Passive activities are less likely to produce flow. As a matter of fact, passive activities such as watching television have repeatedly been found to produce mild depression.

What can a person take away from a conversation about flow? Well, flow comes about in those positive activities where you become totally engaged and lose track of time. It is a very healthy thing to do and, while most people don't associate it with happiness, it most certainly is.

26

The Value of Stress

I once had a client who began our first session with the statement, "I've had too perfect of a life. I'm not prepared for what I'm facing now." And indeed he had been extremely fortunate: good genes, stable loving parents, a marriage to a loving wife for over fifty years. His children, too, were successful and loving. He had had a marvelous, prestigious career filled with enormous rewards and accolades.

All of the above, however, came crashing down when his wife was diagnosed with a serious debilitating illness. Faced with an uncertain and harsh future, my client felt lost, overwhelmed and incapable of managing his everyday affairs.

Given a lifetime of successes, you would think he would be strong enough to manage a severe stress. But his perception was, "I've never been challenged with a really significant personal problem. My parents and wife sheltered me from serious stress, and my job in a major international company protected me from additional life challenges. I can't stand the thought of someone so dear to me failing."

Ironically, my client was making a good point. The stresses of life can be damaging, but they can also provide valuable learning experience. The Dalai Lama has been quoted as saying that "the person who has had more experience of hardships can stand more firmly in the face of problems than the person who has never experienced suf- suffering."

We obviously do not want to court stress, but neither should we deny its value. The pleasures of life gain greater magnitude when compared to past difficulties. Those days of vigor following a long illness are, indeed, treasures, made greater by their contrast with the preceding malaise.

Stress does more than provide comparisons, however. For many it reveals hidden abilities. How often we hear people say, "I could never survive what he or she is going through." But, when the time comes, they do. At first people are frequently numb and their minds and bodies go on autopilot. But from whatever power, they continue to move. After the initial days, they slowly but surely begin anew and, most importantly, they gain in strength. Just as valuable, they recognize that they have survived, sometimes with great courage. Such knowledge is an inoculation for future challenges.

"That which doesn't kill you makes you stronger," Niche's famous quotation is really too global. We know that battle survivors who experience post traumatic-stress syndrome have not been made stronger. There are other examples. But, for most, stress, even severe stress, doesn't exact such an enormous price (although it may not feel that way initially). For the overwhelming majority, the traumas of life are overcome and, in a way, the stress can be beneficial.

Beyond the obvious contrast between sunlight and dark clouds, stress often strengthens friendships. The ties that bind can become stronger. People realize that through rough times there are friends there to comfort and help in the healing process. Then, too, they often reconsider what is important in life. This elevation in sensitivity to life's pleasure and demotion in importance of life's trials can be transforming. For some this conversion is temporary, but for others it is life changing — for the better.

My client? The stresses of a failing spouse came fast. What he hadn't previously learned he now learned quickly. It wasn't easy. It rarely is. But he was smart to seek professional help. He learned that it wasn't a weakness to ask for help from a professional and from friends. He came to value perspective. He treasured the things still present before they were lost. And he came to recognize that he was stronger than he had realized. Was he happy? Well, happy is a relative term. He certainly was happier than he would have been had he not paid attention to what can be learned from the challenges of life. We all are capable of learning, and most of us do just that when we have to.

27

Live in the Present: elsewhere can get you in trouble

I'd had clients who spent their lives endlessly ruminating over past events; perhaps an unsuccessful career, a failed marriage, mean behavior done by them or to them, parents or children who they deemed inadequate, unfair, or just miserable. Other clients were worried about future events: expected failures, pain or humiliation. They were frightened that they wouldn't measure up, that they'll be lonely and destitute.

The fascinating aspect of these two scenarios is that the distressing events are not happening now — in the present. They are happening solely in the person's mind and creating a very uncomfortable emotional state, some level of sadness or depression or alternatively, worry or anxiety. While reducing depression or anxiety is often a complicated effort, there is a general rule of thumb and an antidote to low levels of anxiety and depression — strive to live much of your life in the present.

It's the present, much of it routine, that deserves our consideration. Treasuring the present means taking in details. It means attending to the moment, slowing down time to the now. It means understanding that the "everyday" is a significant part of this treasured experience called life.

Nhat Hanh, the prominent Buddhists teacher, promotes mindfulness, the focus on awareness of everyday experiences. He suggests that we closely attend to such mundane experiences as washing our face, drinking a cup of coffee, feeling the air touch our skin. We need not be spiritual to take his advice. When we attend to the nuances of the human experience, stop and appreciate everyday perceptions, we enhance our well being. We diminish the threats that stem from life's great challenges. Savoring daily experiences protects us from being overwhelmed by the difficulties we inevitably face.

Leo Buscaglio, the popular motivational speaker of the 1980's and 90's, used to tell the story of a man walking by the jungle when out of the brush lunged a tiger. Racing for his life the man found himself between the certain death from the enraged tiger and the drop into a thousand foot canyon. Jumping off the cliff he had a flitting reprieve when he grabbed a branch on the side of the gorge. In the moment before it broke, he reached over and ate a berry within arm's reach.

The story, a parable, may appear silly and without conclusion until one realizes it is meant to say that the man, in the most desperate of circumstances, made the most of the one second left to him, neither focusing upon the past or the future. He experienced that momentary pleasure of the berry.

It is the present, the valuing of everyday experiences, that should occupy the majority of our time, for it makes us most alive. I am struck by how much I enjoy my normal routine after being away from home. Perhaps you feel the same. The everyday experiences with familiar friends, things and tasks now seem a joy. But, unless I work to treasure them, they fade into the background and the pleasure is soon diminished. The pleasure is there, however, waiting for my attention and yours.

So I am determined to write down those daily activities and experiences that I can easily take for granted. I want to spend as much time in the present as I can. "Same old routine," not a problem — there's much to relish.

28

Quiet, Sincere Pride: A pillar of well being

Many people, and even some religions, criticize pride, believing it to be a form of self-centeredness and arrogance. And, of course, it can be if carried to excess. But I take a different view. I believe pride, especially quiet pride, is a source of strength and a pillar of well being.

While we may have been admonished as children "not to get a big head", I find that failure to recall our strengths is more problematic. It's as if the fear of "getting too big for our britches" has kept too many from proudly wearing their britches.

One of the most common challenges that I confront in working with troubled individuals is that they fail to recall their success or just plain survival of an earlier similar problem. They become unable to problem solve, failing to remember the strengths that they brought to bear in similar situations. And one reason they have difficulty recalling those strengths is that they have over-learned the avoidance of vanity, hubris, and arrogance. In the process, they have thrown out or neglected pride.

It is not foolish to take pleasure in your strengths. It's only silly to immodestly broadcast them. But to have them at the ready, to feel the sensation of satisfaction, is not only smart, it's mentally healthy.

There is a simple but effective way to remedy a low level of pride. It is to increase the internal recollection of those things and accomplishments of which you are most proud. It is by creating reminders that stimulate your quiet, but sincere, understanding that you have indeed achieved, loved, taught or in some way accomplished things that are worthy of repeated recall. By increasing the frequency of these recognitions, you move them to a place where they are more accessible during those inevitable troubling times in life.

My personal experience is that people who have a quiet confidence in their abilities, who may know that they are far from perfect, but are nevertheless aware that they are capable of goodness in some form, are able to withstand the disasters that can beset them. But many can benefit from a little work in this area. Here are some examples taken from my life:

Things & Accomplishments of Which I'm Most Proud

1. Trustworthy: When it comes to Jim and Katherine I am always there.

2. Persistence: I got an education against overwhelming odds.

3. Empathy and loving: Mom was a "pip", but I've always cared and supported her.

4. Parenting: I was not perfect, but my daughters were taught some good values and it shows in the people they are today.

5. Intelligence: I was near the top of my class in math.

6. Honesty: I remember that time I returned a wallet with an enormous amount of cash. Some of my friends thought I was foolish, but I never regretted it.

You may not immediately recognize how such recollections can play a role when you are grieving over a loss or anxiously anticipating an upcoming event. But the regular practice of recalling your good personal qualities is likely to make them easily accessible during periods of stress.

I recommend writing out a list of your own sources of pride. I further recommend that you put your list in a place where you will see it daily. If a loved one sees your list, all the better. Sharing is an expression of honest openness — a good quality for a strong relationship.

Don't underestimate how a simple activity like making a list of personal accomplishments and a strong quiet pride can make a difference in your well being.

Exercise

My Sources of Pride

Here are my examples of accomplishments & things of which I'm most proud:

1. Trustworthy: When it comes to Jim and Katherine, I am always there.
2. Persistence: I got an education against overwhelming odds.
3. Empathy and loving: Mom is a "pip" but I've always cared and supported her.
4. Parenting: I was not perfect parent, but my daughters were taught good values, and it shows in the people they are today.
5. Intelligence: I was near the top of my class in math.
6. Honesty: I remember that time I returned a wallet with an enormous amount of cash. Some of my friends thought I was foolish, but I never regretted it.

List your sources of pride below:

Things & Accomplishments of Which I'm Most Proud

1.

2.

3.

4.

5.

29

Finding Well Being and Happiness Through Questions

Most patients who enter psychotherapy are seeking answers. What they are most likely to receive, however, are questions. For questions are powerful windows into the way we think about the world, the manner in which we solve problems and the direction we wish to take. The stereotypic picture of the therapist, from Sigmund Freud to the modern day psychologist in the HBO series "In Treatment", is that of an analytical doctor, musing over the patient's responses. Some truth perhaps, but mostly over-dramatic and simplistic portrayals. The truth part is the careful questioning by the therapist to have the patient reexamine his or her perceptions, helping the patient gather evidence for a healthy functioning life.

Prior to retirement I spent a considerable part of my professional life working as director of an inpatient chronic pain rehabilitation clinic. There we treated patients experiencing a combination of chronic pain, depression and addiction, as well as trained physicians in managing these challenging conditions. You might be surprised to learn one of the fundamental lessons taught to the physicians — not to ask the simple question, "How are you?" This natural opening and empathetic question was counterproductive to our goal of increasing patient activity.

The patient's chronic pain syndrome was worsened by inactivity, magnified by loss of purpose, and increased by attention to pain — all complicated by the daily discussion of pain, especially from that supreme authority, the patient's physician. Therefore, we adamantly required all doctors undergoing training never to utter the question, "How are you?" Instead we required a replacement question, "What have you been doing since I last saw you?"

The contrast between the two questions is significant. The first question draws attention to the patient's pain, reinforces the patient's image of a sick, disabled, nonfunctioning individual — one who is dependent upon others. The substitute question, "What have you been doing since I last saw you?" focuses attention on activity. With that the patient's attention is drawn to the importance of movement, functioning and away from a focus upon pain — all rehabilitation advances.

This little excursion into the world of chronic pain treatment by a behavioral psychologist is meant to reveal, in a small way, the power of questions. The questions we ask ourselves are a window to our world, psychologically and behaviorally. They reveal our thoughts and perceptions.

Struggling patients and unhappy people too often ask

themselves terrible questions, which, of course, result in terrible answers: "Why can't I ever do anything right? What other screw-ups will I make today? Why doesn't she love me?"

Conversely, ask a healthy question, get a helpful answer: "Can I handle the worse case scenario? Have I survived similar situations? What resources do I bring to the problem? What has worked for me before?" Mentally healthy and happy people ask better questions.

Learning to ask the right questions during moments of crisis is a critical skill. But the questions we ask in the course of everyday life are just as important. And it is here, in everyday life, that we can thoughtfully structure questions to stimulate answers to profoundly guide our life and well being.

Here are the questions I have on my computer that I commend to you:

What am I grateful for right now?

What am I enjoying most in my life right now?

What am I committed to in my life right now?

What is my mission in life?

What do I stand for?

These are my questions. I recommend that you examine these, but also create questions that are valuable for you. Place them where you will see them often. Use them as a means of supporting the knowledge that you are living a meaningful life. Use them to maintain emotional stability and a greater sense of happiness.

The questions you ask yourself are every bit as important as the answers that you give.

Exercise

Finding Well Being and Happiness Through Questions

Here are recommended questions:

What am I grateful for right now?

What am I enjoying most in my life right now?

What am I committed to in my life right now?

What is my mission in life?

What do I stand for?

Copy the questions above or create your own similar questions and place them on a sheet of paper, your computer, your ipad or smart phone — wherever you will see the questions on a regular basis. When you come across them, reflect upon your answers.

A variation on the above is to randomly place the questions on a calendar or electronic device so that they appear unexpectedly. I have programmed my questions to appear on my computer calendar monthly for a year in advance.

30

Don't Let The Demons Win

I had one of those days we all have — I couldn't find my car keys and I misplaced my notes for an important meeting. You know, one of those truly frustrating days where nothing seems to go right. I'm generally a happy person, but these little irritations activated my demons.

The demons, in my world as in those of many others, are old feelings of inadequacy, self-criticisms and anxieties that have been repeated over a lifetime. They need have nothing to do with reality. They are simply a well-practiced internal language. You may know them well because they often come out at night. They take familiar form — exaggeration, inappropriate expectations, "stinking thinking" as some psychologists call it. Each of us has our own style of worrying, and these concerns come forward especially after a series of frustrations.

For most of us, the initial response to frustration is often self-blame. "How can I be so stupid as to lose my keys?

Why aren't I better organized — what a dummy." Obviously some people are more prone to such thoughts, but most everyone has, at least, occasional episodes where life seems like pushing mud upstream. When I have such a day, I pull up a series of thoughts that I've written out and placed on my computer for just such an occasion. I'd like to share them with you, but before I do, let me state these are not magical. They take effort. Happiness, as of-often said, takes work. Unhappiness is the default setting that we stay in if we don't take action. That is just one reason to have a plan that you can call upon when the day gets heavy. Here are my reminders:

1. Ultimately I'm responsible for my mood. Yes, it's been a bad day with a series of unfortunate events but they can happen to anyone. This just happened to be my day. It's not the events that are causing my mood. It's what I'm making of them.

2. "This too will pass." How many bad moods have I had in my lifetime? Many, of course. They have all passed and they pass even faster when I take action. In any event, I'll probably feel good tomorrow morning as I usually do.

3. My upset is over things that, in the big picture, are tiny. Get perspective. These events are not changing the course of my life.

4. Look to my strengths. I'm a persistent, strong person who has managed some very substantial challenges in life.

These are my thoughts. Over the years they have stayed basically the same, especially the ones alluding to taking personal responsibility. I know, however, that a bad mood can be very challenging. It's not easy to talk yourself out of one, and I may have to struggle to get myself to my list. But when I do, my mood begins to lift. My list is my list. Yours can be quite different (although I strongly advise you to include taking personal responsibility).

You may already have a plan. Whatever ideas you use, write them out. Happy people get down. They just don't stay down as long as unhappy people. They don't let the demons win.

31

Catch Them "Doing Good"

Bertram R. Caruthers was incredible, a principal of an all black elementary school in the 1960's, the supreme authority in the kingdom of 1,000 children and 30 or so teachers. He was also my first boss; me, white in an otherwise darker pool of marbles.

In an era of strict corporal punishment Principal Caruthers practiced catching the pupils "doing good." A prime example was his approach to tardiness. With many single mothers working two jobs, promptness was hard to achieve. Principal Caruthers attacked the problem by calling up the parents when their child was on time to school or, for that matter, exhibited any other good behavior he observed.

Parents were accustomed to strong-arm principals, authority figures who only called when mischief was afoot. Shocked to hear their principal praising their little one, they, in turn, would startle their child with the news that the principal had called and then share in the pleasure of their child's good report. What a change in atmosphere. What a change in focus.

An interesting part of the "catch them doing good" approach was what it did for the school. It was contagious and instructive for the teachers. Their history was also expecting the principal to lay a heavy hand on misbehaving children, something Principal Caruthers very, very rarely did. His method changed the prism through which most teachers viewed their students and, in the process, gave a clear message of what was expected.

One of my favorite observations in watching Principal Caruthers was his use of the earshot technique. Simply put, the idea was not only to praise children directly, but also to praise the child to someone else *within* earshot of the child. Imagine how you would feel if you overheard your principal telling a teacher what a clever child you were or what potential you had. Powerful!

Catching good behavior is a healthy habit for adults as well, and a practice that ensures a healthy attitude. When we are primarily sensitive to the annoying behaviors and the inconveniences of life, we set ourselves up to be unhappy. On the other hand, when we are prepared to catch others "doing good" we immediately promote a positive perspective. It's not just that we're influencing someone else's behavior, we're modifying our own. We're telling someone else exactly what we like, a benefit to clear communication, and simultaneously ringing up another item for which to be grateful. In the course of a day, a week, a month we are setting the stage for an upbeat attitude.

We know that negative remarks have more sustaining power than positives. Consequently, "catching good" serves to specify your wishes and also builds that reservoir (what I have previously called The Emotional Bank Account) that is the cement of strong relations.

In psychologist John Gottman's book, *The Science of Trust: Emotional Attunement for Couples,* he suggests that building trust comes about in part by building affection and respect within relationships. He argues that there are two parts to nurturing fondness and admiration; first by scanning our world for things to admire and appreciate. He notes that this is the opposite of the critical mind that is most sensitive to errors — very similar to Principal Caruthers' looking for good instead of looking for mischief. Then, Gottman suggests that the admiration and appreciation need to be expressed; they can't remain hidden. Expressing the admired behavior might go like this: "Thank you for noticing how tired I was. You're really sensitive to things like that and I really appreciate it." Actively and overtly building a culture of appreciation and respect is a sign of a good marriage or friendship.

By the way, have you noticed that good marriages use the earshot technique that I spoke of earlier? I doubt they've ever heard it called such, but they are proud of their partner and will often say in their partner's presence how impressed and appreciative they are of their spouse, "Boy, do I have a clever wife" or "My husband is a genius at solving problems."

Principal Caruthers was a smart and clever man. I respected and admired him greatly. I wish he were here now for me to tell him so. He died in 2002 shortly after his old elementary school was named after him.

32

Experience Trump Material Goods

There are fascinating data to show that, in spite of the abundance of new conveniences and greater wealth, Americans are less happy then they used to be. The wealthy have advantages hardly imagined a short time ago. Middle-class homes are replete with multiple cars and technological gadgetry, and many of the poor have a number of televisions and cell phones. Materially we are all better off. So why the decline in well being?

America's surprising downward emotional trend has many causes, but one of the most basic is quite straightforward: happiness stemming from the purchase of material goods doesn't last. Sure the new car smell, the glitter of jewelry, the crispness of new clothes, even the pleasure of a new appliance are initially positive, sometimes joyful, but the pleasure soon fades. Scientists call this "hedonic adaptation". It simply means that we become accustomed to new things. They lose their excitement.

While new possessions don't bring long lasting happiness, experiences are another matter. In the long run, experiences and the memory of them have greater heft, they matter more. It's no surprise that our picture albums are filled with experiences, not objects. Even that picture of your favorite car is valued for your experiences with it rather then its possession. And who has a picture of furniture, jewelry, appliances or clothing in their albums?

Possessions don't have deep lasting pleasure. When psychology professor Ryan Howell asked 154 participants about purchases within the last three months, either material or experiential, acquired with the intention of making themselves happy, experiences led to more happiness than material goods.

Experiences tend to be shared repeatedly. In doing so they often express deep-seated emotions coupled with bonds to others. Even uncomfortable or miserable experiences have staying power. That interminable wait in the airport or the trip with wall-to-wall rain become a part of our life story. And then there are the humorous events that become funnier with the telling. Get lifetime friends together and the stories, told many times, become an emotional ritual of sharing.

Stories save us. When we reshape the story, exaggerating the negative to implicitly illustrate what a brave, stalwart fellow we are, we enjoy the empathy that we feel from others. We receive the gift that others care for us.

Of course experiences also entail real pleasure, new stimulation, and personal accomplishments. Running the rapids, climbing a mountain, sharing time with friends, all entail recollections that give us an emotional "hit." Psychologists have repeatedly shown that our thoughts, even pleasures long since passed, stimulate the pleasure neurons excited in the original experience. The result is that experiences have a long half-life. They are resuscitated to give us repeated pleasure. In doing so they are a reservoir to be savored at will.

Additionally, experiences typically are done with others and thus a sense of relatedness to others — getting closer to friends and family — may be one of the reasons why experiences generate more happiness.

The contrast between possessions and experiences is easily tested. Ask friends to recall something memorable in their lives and you'll find they virtually always center on experiences, usually events involving other people.

Happiness is most related to our internal dialogue. If that dialogue includes a wealth of experiences you have turned into a positive narrative, then happiness is likely your companion. Possessions can leave you feeling lonely.

33

What's Really Important?

It's often said that, on their deathbed, no one wishes they had spent more time at work. Perhaps so, but what do they wish? A probable answer is that they want a loved one to be near. In those final hours or whenever we truly think about what we hold most dear, our relationships are most important.

This point was illustrated in a teaching assignment I shared many years ago. The goal was to create a sense of empathy in new medical students for the patient who was dying.

The medical students were given nine blank cards and asked to write down the names of three people, three material objects, and three personal characteristics that they most valued, listing one per card. So a student's cards might show: computer, car, class ring, mom, dad, girlfriend, integrity, honesty and kindness. They were then asked to stand in a circle and, as their turn arose, to throw a card into the center, representing losing that item while retaining what was left. Little emotion was expressed early in the exercise when most gave up material items such as a car, but emotions rose significantly as the end of life came nearer and they had to decide between their personal integrity and a loved one. This all too real scenario caused many a medical student to break down, even though it was merely an exercise.

It is obvious that material things would be the first to go. No one would find an object to be more important than a close relationship. There may be some cherished objects that hold special memories or symbolize a special event, but most objects pale in comparison to the value we place on our intimate relationships. When the choice was between giving up a personal value such as integrity or a dear friend or relative, the imaginary exercise came too close to home. The emotional toil was significant and the role-playing pushed many into the teacher's intended purpose — to empathize with the emotions and difficult challenges faced by those close to the end of their lives.

Most of us know that relationships are critical to our emotional health, happiness and well being. We know that those who are married, have many close friends or are in deep relationships tend to live longer than those who are isolated. We know that we are most moved at the loss of those close to us. With all that knowledge it would seem most obvious that cementing our relationships would be our highest priority. Unfortunately, what we know intellectually and what we do are often inconsistent.

This most obvious, but basic observation, has been stated by many authors. One of my favorites is Steven Covey, who makes the argument in his book, *First Things First*. Covey argues that our well being is most enhanced when we make sure that we attend to those things that we cherish *before* focusing on other items in our lives — and, of course, for most of us the most cherished thing is our relationships.

The practicalities of living do not allow us spend all of our time directly on our relationships, of course. We have to earn a living, take care of our physical health, and solve everyday problems. But, that said, there is still a tendency to allow the health of relationships to fall down on the priority list. It's a human and understandable failing. Nevertheless, it is a failing that can be altered by discipline and structure. Putting it on a daily to-do list may seem trite but it's a good first step.

People who are most successful in the game of life attend to those around them. When we make sure that we listen, empathize and care for those we love, we not only give, we receive. Our well being comes back many times. We don't have to wait until our deathbed to seek our most important wish.

34

Wisdom We Should Heed

An extraordinary friend of mine died after battling colon cancer for four years. In writing a book on happiness I could do no better than to share her words.

Five months before her death she wrote that "If I had never gotten cancer, I might have not been able to take the time I have this last few years watching and cherishing the nuances of my sons' growth. And I might have never understood how deep intimacy can grow even deeper by sharing difficult decisions with the one you love most or by being temporarily carried away into a children's story on the yellow brick road of your lover's voice."

Susan made it a practice to pay exquisite and prolonged attention to the present moment, as well as taking a non-evaluative approach to her pain, whether physical or psychological. Such an effort could not have been easy. But with practice Susan found she was able to heighten her sensitivities to things otherwise unnoticed and unappreciated and to diminish some of the baggage that usually accompanies pain. In doing so she gained enormously, often exhibiting a contentment and peace. In her dying years, she influenced countless people. On the face of it, her life was diminishing. Her physical abilities became progressively more restrictive and toward the end her waking hours were limited. But, throughout, her inner life expanded.

Susan made it clear that she was not a saint. Beyond her serenity she had periods of depression and anger, even speaking of how her body was abandoning her. But, like other teachers about life, Susan taught others that dying could be a valuable part of our life's experience and that death can teach us about living.

Dr. Susan Montauk spent most of her professional life advocating and caring for the homeless and mentally disabled in Cincinnati, Ohio. She was an extraordinary testimony to a good life and a life with purpose. In her dying words she spoke of the importance of connecting to those we love.

Dame Cicely Sauders, the founder of Hospice, the treatment program that provides palliative care for end of life patients, related a similar thought-provoking sentiment. During a speaking tour in the United States she was asked about her wishes for her own death, to which she replied: " . . . that she would prefer to die with a cancer." Her wish for cancer was, in part, the wish to have the time to connect with those friends and loved ones in her life before her death, to forgive and reminisce. She got her wish.

My friend Susan ended one of her last emails to her friends like this: "I urge those of you who have your health to take a day or two off, perhaps in the woods or by the shore, and perhaps with a significant other, and "pretend" you have only a year to live. Who do you want to get closer to? Who do you want to help? Who do you want to forgive?"

The voices of those near death should be given special attention, for the clutter of life is often swept away, leaving wisdom that is worth heeding.

35

Happy With What You Have

Most of the time messages in Chinese fortune cookies are silly, but once in a while you find a real pearl like, "If you don't enjoy what you have, how could you be happier with more?" Albert Einstein expressed it similarly, "There are two ways to live. You can live as if nothing is a miracle. You can live as if everything is a miracle." However you say it, appreciating the nuances of life is an enormous boon to happiness. It turns out that such sentiment is supported by anecdotes and research alike.

Enjoying what you have means appreciating the little things: that lovely juice or coffee you drink every morning, transported around the world to your local store, available at your pleasure — amazing, wow! Silly to some, perhaps, but actually one of the differences between happy people and those not so happy.

Of all the quotes related to this subject, perhaps my favorite comes from Benjamin Franklin, "Human happiness comes not from infrequent pieces of good fortune, but from the small improvements of daily life." Waiting for that grand event or worrying about possible catastrophes consumes an inordinate amount of many people's lives, whereas those who focus on everyday pleasures do very well, thank you. Except for those who are really struggling to survive, there appears to be little difference in the happiness levels of those in the lower, middle and upper socioeconomic strata.

You might think that having more would bring greater pleasure. While it is true that there is much pleasure in the finer things of life, from amazing technology to world travel to delicious food, we Americans are often obsessed with more. But it hasn't necessarily contributed to our well being. Compared to the 1960's, we have significantly more purchasing power, education, nutrition and availability of entertainment. Yet, according to researcher Martin Seligman, depression is ten times more prevalent, and the first episode of depression strikes an average of 15 years earlier. Many other studies have documented that the nation's happiness level has not increased relative to the country's material gains.

So here is the paradox. Acquisitions often do bring pleasure. Of course, a good deal of the joy is diminished as the newness wears off. But, to be fair, there are some new things that are treasured and desirable. The problem arises when we get caught in the trap of seeking and comparing with others. When newness becomes a goal, even an addiction, when our happiness is dependent upon the acquisition of new things, seeking more is a problem. Appreciating what we have is a safeguard against the pull of acquisitions.

The importance of where we place our focus is well illustrated in our senior population. With advancing age the elderly often experience an increase in ailments and diminished physical abilities. However, even as they must manage previously unknown physical issues, they see others around them who are worse off, and, by comparison, are grateful for the abilities that they have. It is this appreciation of what they have that, surprisingly to many, makes the senior population one of the happiest of any age.

Like many aspects of happiness, the critical feature is your attention. If you were to write down each day the little events that bring a smile to your face you would, in no time, have a treasure chest of pleasures. Discontent often comes from wanting more and not receiving it. Contentment arises mostly from an appreciation of what we have already.

36

When Labeling Yourself, Be Specific and Objective

How we view ourselves has much to do with our sense of well being. When we perceive ourselves as competent, kind and fair, we are likely to be comfortable and compassionate with our self-talk. The labels that we place on ourselves matter. That is why we should be extremely careful and generous in how we internally describe ourselves, taking the utmost care with our self-identity.

Labels need to be accurate. They need to be specific and objective. I knew a woman who walked with a cane and simply stated it as such. She did not perceive herself as disabled, a term she felt diminished and in no way described her abilities. It was true that she walked with a cane, but to her the term "disabled" connoted so much more. She would have no part of it. And, of course, she was right. She was extremely capable, able to engage in a number of vigorous sports and would not tolerate a label that did not provide her a full measure of who she was. Walking with a cane accurately described her situation, no more, no less. This is an example of a careful, healthy self-description.

Walking through our hospital ward one day, I came upon a patient in treatment acting very excited and happy. I went up to her and said, "My, you're ebullient this morning." Surprised, she asked, "What's ebullient?" "Oh ebullient means, full of energy, alive, excited and happy." That same day I overheard a staff member asking my patient, "What got into you today?" "I'm ebullient," replied the patient. And she was that day, aided by a label that reinforced her feelings. Even on a short-term basis, the label that people give themselves — old, fat, out of shape, worthless, inadequate, stupid — makes a difference. In the short term these self-denigrations are little irritations to your system that play a role in your overall well being. When the labels are positive they too play a role, helping set you into a condition of well being.

Labels produce expectations, and expectations influence behavior. One of the best illustrations of this point comes from a study ultimately labeled the Pygmalion Effect, a term borrowed from the play by George Bernard Shaw in which a professor's high expectations radically transformed the behavior of a lower-class girl. The experiment, conducted by psychologists Rosenthal and Jacobson, gave intelligence tests to all of the students at an elementary school at the beginnings of a school year. They randomly placed 20% of the children in classes without any relation to their test results. Importantly, the researchers then confided to the teachers that these 20% of students were showing "unusual potential for intellectual growth" and could be expected to "bloom" in their academic performance by the end of the year. The study conclusively showed that the "intellectual bloomers" showed greater intellectual advancement than those children not so labeled. The change in the teachers' expectation had influenced the performance of the "special" children.

The teachers' expectations undoubtedly conveyed a message to the students in a myriad of subtle ways. This message eventually modified the students' own self-labels, their behavior and the amount they learned.

Take the time to be objective and specific in how you label yourself. I am fat is tremendously different than "I am 20 lbs. overweight." It may not seem much of a difference in language but the former is demeaning and dejecting while the latter is objective and implicitly states a goal. Similarly, "I am stupid" is quite different than "I have a difficult time with that area." The former is global and, once again, damaging, while the latter is more specific and recognizes that there are areas in which you have strengths. The language of self-labels has the power to destroy. It also has the power to build and create. Taking the time to examine how you truly perceive yourself is time well spent.

37

Work On Building Trust

You might not be surprised to hear that a high correlation exists between trust and well being — that is, those who tend to be trusting also tend to experience more happiness. Of course, those who tend to be distrustful tend to experience less happiness.

On an international level the correlation is striking. For example, countries such as Norway, Sweden, Switzerland, New Zealand and Australia that consistently rank at the top of measures of happiness and well being, all rank high in trust. In Norway, 74% say other people can be trusted. Surveys strongly suggest that the Aussies trust their government, and the Danes have overwhelming faith in their government and in each other.

At the same time, those countries in the lowest quadrant of happiness rankings — Sudan, Uganda, Zambia, Rwanda and Niger — are ripe with corruption and mistrust. The citizens of these countries tend to mistrust others and certainly distrust their government.

There are many reasons a country ranks high in happiness, but some characteristics consistently stand out. A stable democracy, a reasonable standard of living, freedom of the press and a strong sense of personal freedom are most prominent. Trust in others and in government is also dominant. Why should that be so? To understand why, consider the opposite feeling — distrust.

Distrust has many underpinnings. Those who feel distrust are likely to be plagued with pessimism, anxiety, fear, anger, blame or an unwillingness to accept personal responsibility, all of which undermine a sense of control. If a person believes that his destiny and fortune are not under his control, it becomes very difficult to maintain a high level of happiness. Distrust is an antecedent to conflict, anger and, on the national level, war.

Trust, by contrast, involves characteristics largely the opposite: optimism, gratitude, empathy and a strong sense of personal control and responsibility.

The picture of trust internationally is consistent with what we feel on a personal level. People who feel comfortable around others and who have faith in the goodness of others tend, on average, to be happier. Those who believe mischief is lurking around every corner and suspect both small and grand conspiracies are prone to pessimism, anxiety, blame, fear and anger. And obviously, beliefs that place personal well being in the hands of others leave little room for confidence and safety.

Like many of you, I have friends with whom I immediately feel comfortable. I know that they respect my thoughts, care about my well being and will support me during good times and bad. I trust them. When I am around them, I am happier in part because I feel safe. They know I am not perfect, but they accept my failings. Experiencing this trust I, too, work to generate similar feelings in them. I respect their views, accept their foibles and work for their well being.

Trust takes work. It requires sensitivity to the feelings of others and a willingness to be vulnerable. It demands that you put yourself out, making yourself available to others during difficult times. It requires that you allow others to care for you as well, something those afraid to be vulnerable are often unwilling to do. It requires you to understand that people are complex and in order to gain someone's trust you must accept them as they are. All very difficult. But then again we know that happiness takes work. Building trusting relationships is one of those treasures worth the effort.

38

Taking Control During Financially Stressful Times

During financially difficult times it is especially easy to believe that we would be happier if we had a boatload of money or at least a boat that wasn't leaking so fast. And while it is true that we wouldn't be thinking about money so much if we weren't loosing money hand over fist in the stock market or seeing the value of our assets melt away like ice-cream on a hot day, it is important to realize that our happiness is truly *not* tied to our financial state (beyond the ability to meet basic survival needs).

You don't believe me? OK, let's take a little trip to Qatar, a little kingdom in the Middle East where the citizens are flush with money. Gasoline sells for fifty cents a gallon, water is free, as are electricity, health care and education. College students are paid a small salary, and when a Qatari man gets married, the government gives him a plot of land to build a house as well as an interest-free mortgage. On top of that, he receives a monthly allowance of roughly seven thousand dollars. You might assume that such benefits are the result of high taxes, but in this oil rich State the opposite is true. Qataris aren't burdened with taxes at all. No income tax. No sales tax. Nothing. So are these affluent citizens happy? Well, according to world measures of happiness, Qatar ranks number 48, just four above Cuba.

Perhaps you don't care what's happening in some far off culture; you see your security and the picture of your remaining life withering away. Remember, if we become obsessed with what we don't have or what we are losing, we surely *will* be unhappy. If we forget what we do have and instead focus on the negative, forgetting to put our financial challenges in perspective, then we *will* be miserable. If we focus primarily on our own difficulties and don't reach out to others, then again, we *will* wallow in our stress. These are our choices. As much as the actual financial difficulties we face can be troubling, it is the that we think about them that makes the difference. As John Milton said, "The mind is its own place, and in itself, can make heaven of Hell, and a hell of Heaven."

By the way, have you always have a lot of money? If you're like me, there were some pretty penny-pinching times and, for me at least, some of the *best* times in my life — real evidence that happiness is only loosely tied to money at best.

Pep talks, even good advice, won't change your misery if you don't follow-up with action, and there are a ton of things you can do to reduce your obsessing. Here are just a few: 1) Write out in detail the times in your life when you were the poorest, what you gained from it, and the happy moments during that time. 2) Go out and do some volunteer work with others far needier than you. 3) Daily write out at least two things for which you are grateful.

Just a few suggestions, but without taking action you can't put all the blame on the external forces.

Robert Pawlicki, Ph.D.

Exercise

Steps to take during difficult financial times

1. Write out in detail the times in your life when you were the poorest.

    a. What did you gained from this experience?

    b. What were the happy moments during the financially difficult time?

2. Make a list of possible volunteer work you might do with others far needier than you.

    a.

    b.

    c.

3. Daily list at least two things for which you are grateful (see previous exercise on gratitude).

39

Thinking Makes It So

You would be hard pressed to persuade most people that events in their lives have little to do with their happiness. But that's what most experts conclude — events have very little to do with happiness. And it's not just modern research on well being that has come to that conclusion. It's evident in the writings of the great sages in world history. In the Far East, Buddha suggested, "Our life is the creation of our mind." The famous Greek philosopher, Marcus Aurelius, wrote, "The whole universe is change and life itself is but what you deem it." During the Renaissance John Milton argued, "The mind is its own place, and in itself, can make Heaven of Hell, and a Hell of Heaven."

In modern Cognitive Behavioral Therapy, a form of psychotherapy, the basic assumption is, "It's not the events of the world, it's your interpretation of the events that create your emotions." Why is it that both science and the great thinkers of the world believe that events are not the drivers of happiness?

I often ask the following question in working with clients: "Is there another person who has remarkably similar circumstances to you and is happy?" The clients, typically and begrudgingly, admit that someone else may have a difficult husband, wife, boss, or relative or is suffering significant financial loss, or is even experiencing chronic pain, but is happier than they. With that answer we can loosen up the belief that their particular situation always causes misery. We can begin to make progress in reducing the stranglehold that misery has on a person. We can then discuss what it is that differs between one person and another in roughly the same situation. The answer inevitably becomes how we interpret the situation, just as the philosophers through the ages have noted.

If you doubt the above, consider the following: legendary British physicist Stephen Hawking was diagnosed in his early 20s with a motor neuron disease that left him trapped in a shell of a body. Now 63, confined to a wheelchair and speaking through a mechanical voice instrument, he is best know for his study of cosmology, the study of the universe, with particular emphasis on quantum gravity, as well as having written the best selling science book of all time. When recently interviewed, he was asked what kept his spirits up. He replied, "My expectations were reduced to zero when I was 21. Everything since then has been a bonus."

Accepting that a person's thinking about an event is a critical variable doesn't, however, change how they perceive things. It's just a starting point. However, if I accept that my interpretation, my perception, is tied to my emotional state, then I can at least be open to a discussion. If, on the other hand, I believe that my anger, depression, anxiety, whatever, is entirely a result of someone or something else, then I'm at a dead end. Since others are mostly outside of my control, I have little realistic hope of changing my misery.

The idea that the events around us are not the sole or critical factor controlling our happiness is a difficult concept to fully accept. After all, don't we feel happier when we are properly sheltered, fed, socially supported and sexually satisfied? Of course we do and, of course, we seek things that provide us with pleasure. None of the scientists or philosophers spoken of denies that we are hard wired to seek pleasure, in its myriad forms, and to avoid pain. Nevertheless, the filter through which we experience our positive and negative input, determines our emotional state. It is that filter, our individual perception, that is so important.

So seek pleasure. Avoid pain. You have no choice but to do so. (Even the masochist who loves to feel pain is an illustration of how our perceptions really dictate our experience.) We all know that "one man pleasure is another man's pain." But always, always, recognize that it's your interpretation of what is happening around you that will rule your happiness. Such a belief frees a person from blaming others and thereby losing control. Accepting that your interpretation plays a critical role in your well being moves you into maturity and control. As Shakespeare said, "There is nothing either good or bad, but thinking makes it so."

40

Controlling What You Can Control: What alternative do you have?

About fifteen years ago I conducted a series of lectures and discussions in two state prisons. Walking into a maximum-security prison is an incredible experience. Your television images are probably somewhat accurate — the harsh, cold, dehumanizing environment and the incredibly small cells are there before your eyes. What you cannot fully sense on your television set is the daily fear, the lack of privacy, the constant noise, the loneliness and the danger. Men in this severe environment vary widely in their ability to cope. Most remarkably, some are happy — happier than at any other time in their lives. I repeatedly asked prisoners "Is it possible to be happy in prison?" I never heard any prisoner say no even though everyone said it was difficult.

When I share this information, surprise is the most common reaction. The loss of freedom in the austere dangerous prison environment, void of the people and things we love, seems a hardship unbearable to manage. And yet this most harsh existence is, for some, a place where satisfaction is found. The men who were the most successful had found a little niche that they could control in sea of experiences beyond their control.

Most prisoners were not happy, but some were, and others were happier than they had been outside of prison. Once again, the point being that so much of happiness has to do with our internal dialog.

There are many, many people who make their own prison, with walls created of fear, anxiety or depression. These emotions, typically fueled by distorted thinking, limit constructive behavior, because they interfere with problem solving. Whether it's a health, relationship, financial or the myriad of other problems that are a part of life's struggles, an early question in managing debilitating emotions should be "What part of this situation can I control?" Among the many benefits of asking this question is that it takes us away from one of the most destructive ways of approaching personal problems — blaming.

Blaming is seductive, for it often comes with a benefit — temporary avoidance of looking at our responsibility in the situation. This temporary advantage comes at a substantial cost, however. It puts constructive problem solving out of our control and control into the hands of others — often the very people we would least like to be in charge of our emotional state. Blaming also creates anger, rarely a favorable emotion, as well as interfering with moving onto more pleasant endeavors.

It's interesting to remind ourselves of the stories that we

hear of people facing incredible hardships, the Michael J. Foxes of the world. When we analyze how these heroic individuals not only survive but also have thrived, we realize that their internal dialog is not filled with blame or regret. Like the oft-cited Serenity Prayer, they took some of life's most extreme challenges, accepted the part they couldn't control and worked on controlling what they could. It is a lesson that we need to remind our selves of, day after day after day. Move away from blame, control what you can control — a major step in creating a happier life.

The Serenity Prayer

God grant me the serenity to accept the things I cannot change; courage to change the things I can; and wisdom to know the difference. —

Reinhold Niebuhr

Exercise

Controlling What You Can Control

List your two most vexing problems.

1.

2.

For each of these, list what you can control and what you cannot.

Problem 1

Can control	Cannot control
1.	1.
2.	2.
3.	3.

Problem 2

Can control	Cannot control
1.	1.
2.	2.
3.	3.

41

Jump for Joy Happiness

In contrast to a general high state of happiness, there are the rare but treasured times when we are incredibly elated. One of those moments in my life was most revealing. My bout of ebullience occurred at the end of an eight-month journey with four other committed committee members, working on the task of securing a new minister for our church. Those who have travelled this road know the endurance and intensity required to reach the finish line. We met every week and worked an average of 15 hours a week, spending more time with each other than some of us spend with our spouse. So with such a long investment, mildly analogous to giving birth, the culmination was suspenseful and anxiety filled. Not only was the "birth" greatly sought, but also the thought of being "pregnant" another year highly feared.

When the child was born, oops, I mean the minister of our choice accepted, I yelled, screamed, jumped off the floor and rushed to share with family, friends and anyone within earshot. My face flushed, my pulse jumped and I felt terribly alive — not an everyday feeling of happiness but a rare, memorable occasion that will find a place-mark in the significant events of my life.

When I quieted a bit, I realized that this was one of the few times in my life when I literally jumped for joy. And so, being in the "happiness business" I decided to track how long the feelings would last.

Obviously the jumping up and down ceased, as did the flushing and high pulse rate. But the euphoria continued for two or three days. During that time I enthusiastically shared the good news with everyone I met, casual friends and strangers. I found myself smiling, replaying the de-tails and again feeling physically excited. My sleep was peppered with awakenings with my mind happily bub-bling. Awake, there was energy in my step and a glow around everything else. Irritations seemed trivial and short lived.

By the fourth day I encountered my first return to reality — someone was rude and intrusive, enough to cause my anger to engage. This was more glaring because of the contrast to the semi-giddy state in which I had been liv-ing. I expressed my displeasure and emotionally moved on, not immediately, but probably faster than if a bed of good feelings had not cushioned the anger.

Some time passed and the elation subsided. The glow was there but as a softer ember. My daily routine re-turned with the accompanying challenges and irritations. My mind flitted back to the excitement of a few weeks earlier but was now focused on everyday routine. Super happiness cannot be held.

So what have I learned from my observations? The emotional high was fantastic: a physical and psychological rush. It was made more glorious and extended by sharing it with others. It was time limited.

It's understandable why some are addicted to the adrenalin hit, the extraordinary thrill. But addiction, even a super happiness addiction, is not where I want to go. It took extraordinary commitment to reach the "jump for joy" state and, while I admire those who are dedicated enough to achieve life's highs, I want to make sure that I treasure the moments in between. In our modern life there are many who aspire for celebrity status, assumedly attaining a super happy state of supreme adulation. They delude themselves by wanting such a transitory moment to be permanent. I want to make sure that I treasure the day-to-day experiences, and making the most of the routine of life, for that is where I, inevitably, will spend 99% of my life.

We are hard wired to acclimate to pleasures. A few servings of ice cream or chocolate is wonderful, a constant diet of either would soon grow tiresome (although some would contest this assertion, especially the chocolate). The same is true with super emotional highs. It's their very rarity that makes them special. But waiting for them to appear in order to feel happy would be a major mistake.

42

Keeping Worry at Bay

Mark Twain famously said, "Ninety-eight percent of what I worried about never happened." It appears to be an all too common trait to worry and fret about what might happen. Like Mark Twain, it's also true that we generally worry needlessly, or at least more than necessary. We project the worst and, in the process, often create more unhappiness than misfortune itself.

Worrying is a challenge, but there are some time-tested approaches that can soften the anxiety. Here are three of my favorites:

> 1. Gain perspective by going back in time to the most challenging moments in your life and recalling not just the problem that was faced but the deep-seated fear. Recall how you initially may have felt paralyzed, perhaps overwhelmed. And then remember how, in spite of some initial feelings of helplessness,

you gathered strength and moved forward. Search for perseverance, intelligence, and diligence — whatever it was that carried you through the difficult time. These strengths are likely to still be available as a resource if given a chance to be resurrected. If any of these characteristics are part of your core image, they are likely to be very powerful in disempowering the worry.

2. Turn from oblique worry to creative problem solving. Worry is a form of pain and as such has a dominating effect. It tends to block out competing, often more rational, thoughts. Any effort that interferes with the recycling of irrational thought will have benefit. Confronting the worry is valuable place to begin, but where? One approach is to simply consider the worst possible outcome. This oft-used technique is valuable because it transforms the oblique, vague anxiety into a concrete possibility, thereby making it more susceptible to problem solving.

Viewing the worst possible scenario immediately raises the question of whether you can survive the disaster, and more often than not the answer is yes. Yes, you've been poor, alone, sick — whatever — before. You got through it before and you can get through it again if it happens. It wasn't fun, but you did it. Reminding yourself that you've been there before and have survived takes the wind out of most any `worry's sail.

3. Attend to your internal dialogue. This is a distinction that separates those who deal ef-effectively with life's anxieties and those that don't. Happier people tend to use an internal dialog that differs from the worrier. You hear it in their little self-statements: "I've been down before and I pulled myself out. I'll do it again." "I remember feeling so depressed I didn't want to leave the house." These statements recognize that failure is a part of a normal life. Those who fail to manage their difficulties tend to focus on the present problem, failing to put their problems in perspective. Those who do manage their worries are more likely to be in tune with, "This too will pass."

Happiness takes work. It also takes smarts — the intelligence to incorporate little strategies that prevent sadness and anxiety from getting the upper hand. Gaining perspective is one such strategy, moving from oblique worry to concrete problem solving is another, and paying attention to your internal dialog a third — three approaches that can keep excessive worry at bay. Mark Twain was right. The overwhelming percentage of our worries never come to pass. Being prepared is a good way to manage them when they do appear.

Robert Pawlicki, Ph.D.

Exercise

Keeping Worry at Bay

Write out a particularly bothersome worry in the space below.

1. Gain perspective by remembering a period in your life when you had a worry similar to your current concern.

> a. Write out how you felt emotionally at the time.
> b. What personal strengths did you use to get through the difficulty?

2. Turn from oblique worry to creative problem solving.

> a. Consider the worse possible outcome that could result if your worry came true.
> b. Could you survive such an outcome?
> If the answer is yes, remind yourself that you have survived a similar problem before and can again.

3. Attend to your internal dialogue.

> a. Draw a line down the center of a blank sheet of paper.
> b. Write out your worries as clearly as possible in the left column, highlighting those words that evoke the greatest concerns.
> c. In the right column, write out specific, objective, balanced counter arguments to your worries.
> d. Remind yourself that "This too will pass" or any other phrase that gives you perspective.

43

Happiness and Sex

OK, OK. I can't avoid it any longer: happiness and sex. It's a difficult topic. I've been writing about happiness for years and never once have I written an essay exclusively about sex. I'm guilty. It's a complicated topic, filled with pitfalls. But the truth is that sex is a basic biological need, and engaging in it does make us happy, very happy.

To point: Using a most thorough method of measuring happiness, participants in a study rated everything they did on a previous day with such descriptors as happy, impatient, depressed, worried, tired, etc. on a seven-point scale. The study, conducted with 900 Texas women, resulted in responses of sex, socializing, relaxing, praying or meditating, and eating as the most satisfying in descending order of satisfaction. Exercising and watching TV came next. Again sex ranked number one.

But I suspect that I didn't have to tell you that sex makes people happy and I doubt that citing a study was needed to convince you. From the time that those first adolescent hormones come into play until they disappear, sex is a pleasurable experience. Of course there are times when sex is not available and then, like lack of food is painful, lack of sex is painful. For those moments we may wish that sex were not so important. Then, for some, there comes a time when hormonal factors are diminished and sex no longer plays a dominant role in life. But let's put those times aside and address the fact that we are sexual animals, and for a good portion of our lives sexual satisfaction is a driving force and very relevant to our general happiness.

The discussion of sex is complicated by the obvious fact that sex and intimacy change over a lifetime. The images of raucous, acrobatic sex lessen with the years as physical, circumstantial and psychological needs change. Sex, once thought of as sexual intercourse, is often redefined with age to include the softer, more tender sides of intimacy: holding hands, cuddling, sitting shoulder to shoulder. those couples that do maintain a pattern of sexual intercourse in advanced years, it often decreases in frequency, but is treasured more.

Smart partners know that sex doesn't start in the bedroom, but often in the kitchen, living room or car — not in the manner of sexual images that might come to mind, but in the little daily exchanges of kindness and tenderness in those places. To state the obvious again, sexual excitement and satisfaction are greater for those who share a mutual intimacy fueled by everyday affection. In that sense, bringing a cup of coffee, offering to help with a chore, providing unsolicited praise, giving an affectionate snuggle or the myriad of positive exchanges that happy couples and partners adopt, are really the "foreplay" to a satisfying love life.

Conversely, anger, sarcasm, insults, etc. in the course of the day are toxic to a healthy sex life. Unfortunately, just as fatal is a lack of foreplay — the kind of "foreplay" I spoke of above. When a man or woman does not attend to the kindnesses that increase fondness, it diminishes the quality of the sexual experience and the happiness that we associate with a good sex life is diminished.

So what recommendations can I make regarding happiness and sex? I'll leave the mechanics to the sex therapists, but if you're interested in increasing the frequency and quality of your sexual experience (and the concomitant happiness) look no further than sincerely attending to your loved one with those affectionate words and behaviors that are the real fuel to a good love life.

44

Worth Taking the Time to Create: A smile file

For many years I have kept a "smile file" to ward off pro-longed sadness. The file comes into play when I am feeling down, maybe a little depressed. In it are the accumulated "pleasures" of my life, the highlights, accomplishments, awards and the appreciations of other people. The signifiers of close friendships are, perhaps, the most important. It's nice to reach some of life's more challenging goals, but it's the relationships that bring the warmest feelings to the fore. When I return to my accumulated memories, I feel an upward bump in my emotions.

I am, for the most part, an optimistic, happy, engaged person, rarely feeling more than the regular dips of life. But occasionally the dips migrate into a mood that sends out a signal that action must be taken. I have often taught that sadness, anxiety, even anger, are useful human emotions. It is only when these emotions are allowed to linger, even fester, that our mental health is in peril. Happy people and those with a good state of emotional health are, by contrast, expert in taking personal responsibility for their emotions. They know how to truncate or reduce bad feelings, preventing them from expanding into a depression.

Everyone wants to be happy, but learning *how* to be happy is another matter. Sure it's possible to pass out bromides like "think positive," "get a good attitude" or, one of the most silly in my opinion, "shape up." My experience, however, is that few people respond to such notions. It's not that anyone purposely wishes to wallow in sadness. It's more often that people lack tools to right their emotional boat. That's where a smile file comes into play, one of many little actions that interfere with depression taking hold. I use it as a tool to cap feelings of sadness, preventing the feelings from lingering.

Here are a few examples of scraps of paper found in my smile file: "You have been a major influence in my life" — a comment made decades ago that would likely be lost to my memory if not recorded and recalled through my file. There are many comments from clinical psychology students (e.g., "I've learned so much from you.") that I mentored during their internship — comments that can bring a glisten to my eyes still. Then there are the numerous remarks noting sensitivity and caring, characteristics that I treasure and that feed my identity. Because I have kept this file for over twenty-five years it provides not just snapshots but a lifetime film of events and most importantly, relationships.

Over the years I've turned to my smile file during times when I've begun to feel low. I've also used it proactively. I've inserted random reminders in my calendar, say three times a year. When those dates pop up, I rummage through my file and inevitably get an emotional lift.

Scientifically we know that those who rate high in gratitude, perspective and acceptance tend to be happy. In its own way my smile file stimulates all three. Filled as it is with a myriad of warm remarks from close friends and peers I can again gain a sense of from recognizing my good fortune, understanding that my daily inconveniences are simply a part of life, and appreciate that life has ebbs and flows that I must accept. A smile file — I highly recommend starting one.

Robert Pawlicki, Ph.D.

Exercise

Create a Smile File

A smile file is a collection of material that reminds you of friends, deeds, accomplishments, humorous events, relatives or awards that lifts your spirit.

1. Search your home for letters, awards and notes that provide you with a sense of personal comfort and pleasure.

2. Begin paying attention to those compliments that you receive and write them down, noting the people and the date.

3. Place all such written notes and any other items that serve the purpose of bringing pleasure to you in a file marked Smile File.

4. Place memos on your calendar, electronic or otherwise, reminding you to peruse your smile file.

45

Taking Some of the Negative Out Of Uncertainty

We've all been there — in a waiting room, anticipating news, hoping for the best, fearing the worse. It's a very trying situation, avoiding thoughts of what could happen, keeping a calm face while stifling our fears.

It turns out that uncertainty is much more stressful than the most damaging news. The news itself can be dealt with, whereas uncertainty leaves us frustrated and confused.

An experiment in the Netherlands illustrates the point. Subjects were given 20 electrical shocks. One group received 20 intense shocks while another group received 17 mild shocks and three unpredictable intense shocks. The subjects who were uncertain when they would receive the intense shocks sweated more profusely and their hearts beat faster. A team of researchers at Emory University examined these reactions and found that some dreaded the anticipation so much that they chose a more powerful early shock than to wait.

Likewise, in a study of patients who had undergone colostomies 6 months earlier, a situation more realistic to human experience, those who learned that the situation was permanent were actually happier that those who thought that they might someday be returned to normal. Similar results have been found in other diseases such as neurogenerative disorders. In all of these studies bad news turns out to be less problematic than uncertainty.

Why is uncertainty worse than bad news? Primarily because we can deal with bad news and then move on. We get busy adjusting our attitude and behavior. We take a deep breath, pull up the proverbial bootstraps and plan our future. Uncertainty, on the other hand, strands us in the present, waiting.

Ironically what we fear most, while uncertain, is often a place we've already been — being alone, poor or dependent, for example. But we tend to remember the difficult parts of such a state and fail to recall either any positives or any of the rewards of growth or recovery. Consequently, feelings loom vague and ominous.

There are constructive actions, however, that can be taken to battle uncertainty. Consider the worse thing that could happen and imagine how you would handle that situation. Create a plan spelling out what you would do if the worst happened. Write it out in as much detail as you can muster. Note similar difficulties that you've overcome in the past. Write down a list of assets and strengths you bring to the situation, including friends and relatives. Contemplate the best possible outcome if the worst were to happen and write out what needs to be done to achieve that end. In other words, plan and take action. Imagining yourself handling the worst possibility in detail is a major step in reducing your worries.

Secondly, voice your fears to someone you trust. Often our fears are replete with exaggerations and distortions eclipsing constructive alternatives. What you don't know makes you nervous and prone to catastrophizing. A friend who has your best interest at heart can shed light on a dark picture and help relieve you of singularly shouldering your deepest fears.

It takes strength to manage uncertainty, but it's a wise choice to take steps that are under your control to gain some sense of well being in a difficult situation.

Robert Pawlicki, Ph.D.

Exercise

Uncertainty

Write out an uncertainly that has been bothering you in the space below.

1. Consider the worse thing that could happen and imagine how you would handle that situation. Write it out as thoroughly as possible.

2. Create a plan spelling out what you would do if the worst happened. Write it out in as much detail as you can muster. Note similar difficulties that you've overcome in the past.

3. Imagining yourself handling the worst possibility in detail is a major step in reducing your worry. Write down a list of assets and strengths you bring to the situation, including friends and relatives. Contemplate the best possible outcome if the worst were to happen and write out what needs to be done to achieve that end. In other words, plan and take action.

   a. Assets

   b. Personal strengths

4. Voice your fears to someone you trust. A friend who has your best interest at heart can shed light on a dark picture and help relieve you of singularly shouldering your deepest fears.

It takes strength to manage uncertainty, but it's wise to take steps that are under your control to gain some sense of well being in a difficult situation.

46

Facing Death Gives Us Life

It may seem that death and happiness shouldn't be in the same sentence. After all, the grim reaper is something we all dread.

However, a thoughtful visit to the idea of your own death can be a healthy trip. If it stimulates attention to life's treasures, if it prompts appreciation of both the grandeur and the subtleties of life, if it encourages thoughts concerning your contribution and legacy, if it brings you closer to others now instead of waiting for later, then it is a worthwhile visit.

For some, the thought of their own death is avoided at all cost. Why think of death? Why not focus on the moment? Why bring discomfort into my life, they ask. As a psychologist, I recognize the value of a certain level of denial and can empathize with such leanings. On the other hand, thinking about death in a measured amount can have the value of bringing awareness of the need for kindness, gratitude, perspective, forgiveness and acceptance to the fore. If such thoughts increase the likelihood of these actions, then the mental contemplation is worthwhile. These are all valuable contributors to well being.

A friend reported that the best time of her marriage was her husband's last year of life. "Every day was like magic," she said. "He appreciated everything, every flower, every smell, every touch. We no longer quibbled over what to eat for breakfast, what movie to go to or trivial things. It was the most glorious time."

Such mental shifts are common among people who have had a life-threatening experience. Their daily routine and denial of their own mortality is shaken, and they are abruptly sensitive to the miraculous feeling of being alive. For a time they often live an altered life, a life treasuring the subtleties, nuances and items such as relationships that are truly what they value most. But the human makeup is such that, over time, even those who have been near death return to a routine during which these thoughts decline. When they disappear altogether, I believe something is lost.

Many people were moved by *Tuesday with Morrie*, a book about a college professor who decided that his own death should be a teaching moment, an experience that he would accept and share. In the author's moving account, Morrie uses his dying as reason to elevate everyday life and relationships, to turn up the volume on beauty, kindness and gratitude. Morrie even decides to have his own funeral, with all of the adulations and tributes, while he's still alive. Thinking about death, he moved forward important items in life.

Death tells us that our life is finite — that we are not totally in control. In this message we, again, have a choice. We can bemoan the sadness of our fate or constructively use the fact to dictate what we do control — our lives.

47

Social Ties: A strong contributor to health and well being

I have often written that social connections contribute to a happier and longer life. But I return to the subject because the research continues to accumulate and reinforce its importance.

One of the most interesting studies was conducted by a Yale epidemiologist and involved 7,000 men and women in Alameda County, California. Over a nine-year period she found that people who were *not* connected with others were three times as likely to die as those who had strong social ties. The type of social tie did not matter — family, friends, church or volunteer groups. But here's the kicker: those with unhealthy lifestyles but close social ties actually lived longer than those with healthy lifestyles and poorer social contact. In other words, strong social contact trumped all the work that goes into maintaining a healthy lifestyle. Of course, those who had *both* strong social support and a healthy lifestyle did the best.

Robert Pawlicki, Ph.D.

The idea that social interactions are a basic ingredient to a healthy existence (and I believe nourish happiness) is a message worth repeating. Often we don't recognize how much the actions of others feed our behaviors and beliefs, but they do. Here are two brief stories that illustrate the point.

Most everyone reaching adulthood before 1961 remembers the burial ceremony of assassinated President John Fitzgerald Kennedy at Arlington cemetery and, most poignantly, the military Taps that capped an already emotional day of deep national sadness. Those Taps were delivered by Sergeant Keith Clark, Principal Bugler of the U.S. Army Band, a man who had performed for President Kennedy several times, including sounding Taps at the Tomb of the Unknowns two weeks earlier. But unlike his flawless performances of the 24 notes at hundreds of ceremonies at Arlington, this occasion was different. He cracked one note in an otherwise perfect routine. This stunning note with its emotional signature signified for many the broken-hearted feeling that permeated those watching. Remarkably, in the following months the missed note took on a life of its own as other buglers at Arlington Cemetery, experts all, also faltered on the same note.

The actions of one person similarly affected others when Roger Bannister broke the four-minute mile record in 1954. The four-minute mile was not merely a record for millennia; it was considered a psychological barrier that represented the limit of human's physical ability. But what is remarkable is that, within one year, 37 other runners also broke the barrier, and the following year another 300 runners broke the four-minute mile. Not only did

Roger Bannister break the physical barrier, he also changed the belief that it could not be done.

These stories are in harmony with the conclusions of Harvard researcher and psychologist, Nicholas Christakis. Dr. Christakis and his team examined massive amounts of data accumulated over decades from the famous Framingham cardiac research. They found that, if your friends are happy, it increases your probability of being happy by 15%. Astonishingly, if your friend's friends are happy, it increases the likelihood that you'll be happy by 10%. Like the stories above, those around us, often without our awareness, affect us more than we realize.

There are lessons to be learned from Dr. Christakis' research. Seek others who are upbeat, positive and happy as much as you can. They will provide you with nourishment. Work to be happy yourself as well. Your happiness will be a gift to those around you. You might actually lengthen their lives. While we can't always be happy, nor can we expect that of our friends, it is a smart person who avoids a heavy diet of those who look at the world through dark glasses. It is wise also to renew yourself with those who look at the world brightly.

48

Listening, Well Being and Happiness

I value the art of listening and those who listen well. But I've never come across a study that links good listening skills and well being, until recently. In a striking study, psychologist and researcher, Larry Scherwitz, taped the conversations of nearly 600 men, a third of whom had heart disease. He then counted how often the men used first-person pronouns — I, my, and me. Those who used them most often were also most likely to have heart disease and, when followed for several years, most likely to suffer heart attacks. Those who were more other-directed, (that is speaking away from I, my and me) and listened, had more favorable outcomes. Dr. Scherwitz advised: "Listen with regard when others talk. Give your time and energy to others; let others have their way; do things for reasons other than furthering your own needs."

There is an implicit kindness embedded in Dr. Scherwitz's advice. Listening can be a gift that you provide to another by giving them your undivided attention, respecting and valuing what they have to say. A rehabilitation doctor who was a friend of mine told me this story many years ago and it struck a chord. One of her patients had a chronic condition that resisted her interventions. After trying every test, therapy and medication she could think of, the physician struggled to tell her patient that there was nothing more she could do and that perhaps he should seek other medical care. No sooner had the words left the doctor's mouth than the patient rushed to say that he had known this was the case for a long time. The patient said that, while he respected her expertise, her medical knowledge was no longer his primary interest. It was the fact that she took the time to listen to him, giving him her full attention, that caused him to seek regular appointments. He assured her that her careful listening was not to be overlooked and, for his part, he had no intention of seeking other medical care.

For over twenty years my professional life included treating patients with serious physical conditions. I'm sure it will not come as a surprise that the complaint I heard most frequently regarding medical care was the lack of listening — this seemingly most simple of acts. On the other hand, those who felt close to their doctor and felt that they were receiving good care almost inevitably said that they felt listened to.

The benefits of listening well are not confined to the patient-doctor interaction. Listening is a critical ingredient in every good relationship. It is most obvious in its absence in poor relationships. Listening is special and being a good listener is a valuable personal asset. It allows you to enter into someone's world and to form a bond unavailable to those who cannot or do not listen well.

Listening is deceptive. It can appear to be easy and automatic, a passive behavior, but it is not. It takes energy, selflessness and certainly attention. To do it well takes sincerity and, at its highest form, empathy. Poor listeners are legion — their minds race ahead to what they wish to say. The worst of them, hardly maintain eye contact and interrupt, leaving the speaker with the empty feeling of-often associated with disrespect.

When real listening occurs, perceptions often change — perhaps not immediately, because personal biases can be strong. But with increased listening, we begin to hear details not originally within our understanding. We begin to see the circumstances and conditions present in the other person's actions. And most importantly, we come to see the other person as a human being. If you wish to elevate your listening skills, pay attention to the emotions behind the words. A careful and tactful insertion of your recognition of those emotions will often bring you to a whole new level of closeness and conversation.

Listening is magical. It brings us into awareness that we all share fears, anxieties, worries and feelings. It can heal. Any behavior with this much power in enhancing and cementing relationships is worth our attention. Listening helps build quality relationships — a critical ingredient in building our own happiness.

49

And You Thought Ecology Only Pertained To The Environment

Over 50 years ago, the word ecology was virtually unknown. Since that time we've all become very acquainted with the word. The dictionary definition is "the relations and interactions between organisms and their environment."

But it has always seemed to me that another ecology should be our ultimate focus — our mental ecology. For that ecology — what is happening between our mental state and our well being, self-worth, problem-solving abilities and happiness, is critically important. You may not have considered the fact that you have some control over this ecology.

The mind's "environment" is made of perceptions, stories, images and processes that all affect the way we interpret new input. Those elements and their balance can be beneficial or harmful. *If* the mind is dominated by trust, optimism, and affection, the results are obvious — new input goes through a filter of generosity, kindness, humor, tolerance and empathy. The person has a high probability of general well being and happiness. *If* the input goes into a mind filled with fears, conspiracies, distrust, suspicion and negativity, it is *unlikely* that happiness will be left much room. If the negatives are well ingrained, the outcome is predictable: depression, anxiety, protectiveness, prejudice, self-centeredness, and various levels of meanness, intentional or otherwise.

Unfortunately, our mental ecology is often little considered. We are frequently passive in accepting whatever pollutants come our way. The 11 o'clock nightly news is a good example, and one of my pet peeves — the flame, blame and disaster list at the end of the day. Not only is it sickening in its selection of negative world events, its timing is critical to do maximum damage — right before most of us go to sleep. If you are concerned about what food you place in your body, you might well want to consider what images you place in your mind.

The world is a challenging place filled with many horri-events. It would be unrealistic to deny either our own or the world's problems. But it is smart, even wise, to examine what amount and type of information can lead to *inappropriate* levels of fear, suspicion, prejudice and anger.

The filter we use to protect our mental ecology is one that recognizes the types and quantity of negatives. Negative, angry, conspiratorial, distrustful, and self-centered people should be allowed in our lives only in small doses and even then their presence should be accompanied by qualifying thoughts. Major sad and catastrophic world events should be thoughtfully considered in the entirety of life's experiences. Positives in any shape, size or intensity should be welcomed, savored and frivolously magnified.

Just as we strive to carefully monitor how much pollution we place in the air, our water and our bodies, it makes sense to honor our minds. For our mind is the core of our being. And yet our most precious asset is often left to the vagaries of others. It's smart and a contribution to your well being to take an active role in creating a healthy mental ecology. A good place to start is to simply examine your daily input from friends, relatives and media, and then make adjustments to achieve a healthy mental ecology.

50

Thank You: It's hard to overdo it

Many years ago, while awaiting some foreign visitors, I browsed through a number of books they had been assigned in preparation for their visit to the United States. The one consistent characteristic, cited repeatedly, was how polite Americans were, and in particular saying "thank you." I really don't know if we, as a population, are more polite than other nationalities, but I am especially enamored with the value of this simple tradition.

Coming from a discipline that examines habits, sequences of behaviors and reinforcers, saying "thank you" is a standout. Since it's so much a part of our culture, you may underestimate its power. And you also may fail to use it as extensively as you might believe. Here are three ways in which a simple, sincere "thank you" is valuable and why it might be worth your extra attention.

First, "thank you" brings gratitude to the forefront of your mind. We know that of all the every day human behaviors, gratitude is one of the most powerful in maintaining a happy state. Gratitude creates an awareness of the positives in our lives and helps combat the power that negative events can have over our emotions.

Scientists who study these matters tell us that it takes at least five compliments to offset a single negative remark, and that pales in comparison to the positives needed to offset many other pains. Consequently, any action that stimulates an awareness of gratefulness is worth its weight in gold. Opportunities to say "thank you" are endless. In doing so, you accumulate little nuggets of awareness that you do, indeed, have a great deal to be thankful for.

One of the most common complaints heard in marital therapy is that "He/she should have known what I wanted. We've been married forever." Marital therapists pull their hair out over this one. Assuming that others know what you are thinking is a dangerous game. It is better to clearly and often state your desires, no matter how strongly you believe those wishes should be obvious. Furthermore, if a behavior rarely occurs and then is not clearly acknowledged, it will continue to happen infrequently.

A sincere thank you can both acknowledge and reinforce. But the behavior doesn't have to be rare to be worthy of a thank-you acknowledgment. Behaviors that you wish to see more often will increase in frequency if you follow them with a thank you: Thank you for putting the dishes away. Thank you for the hard work that you do. Thank you for the loving way you touch me. Thank you for being there to support me. Thank you so much for taking care of me when I'm sick. Thank you for really listening to me. A sincere thank you cements a relationship. It keeps a relationship from becoming stale. It make a spouse, partner, friend feel appreciated. Their sense of well being is likely to come back to you and enhance your life as well.

Saying thank you creates a small but marvelous bonding experience, especially between loved ones and close friends. It increases intimacy. A heart-felt thank you identifies exactly what you want. That may not seem significant, but clear communication is difficult. We need every signpost we can muster. Thank you says, "This is what I like." "This is what I value." Personally, I go out of my way to not only say thank you, but also to expand upon it whenever I have a chance. An everyday encounter with a waiter or waitress for example: "Thank you for bringing our food so promptly; I really appreciate it." Not only does it show my appreciation, it signals what I value without being negative. Imagine how important this habit is in personal relationships.

Anyone reading this book will undoubtedly say that they say thank you often. In a sense, a thank you is a form of a compliment, and studies clearly show that virtually everyone *overestimates* how often they compliment others.

Thank you for reading my book. I have been truly fortunate to have you do so.

Acknowledgements

I suspect that most writers believe they produce pearls of wisdom. My wife, my first reader of choice and primary editor, brought that notion crashing to the floor many years ago. More often than not, those pearls need considerable cultivation before becoming anything close to gem-like. And the pages of red marks initially may come as quite a surprise.

Early in our marriage, my wife, Gail Scarbrough, had to decide, "Do I hold back in using my red editing pen or risk hurting our relationship?" Fortunately for me, she held nothing back and thus enhanced both my writing and our marriage. I am enormously indebted to her for her patience and talent, to say nothing of the enormous amount of red ink she used.

I am very fortunate to have not only wonderful friends but extremely talented ones like Gayl and Dick Glover. Gayl, with her insight and sharp eye, and Dick, with his organizational and photographic skills, were a great help in reframing the final product.

The same can be said of Doris Grieder, my friend of over 30 years. I could say that as a reader Doris found weeds I was too close to see, but that misses her more significant contribution as a supportive friend who has consistently encouraged me to expand my thinking and knowledge.

I would like to express my appreciation to Jan Durham and Tom Williams, who rounded out a team of readers who helped polish the manuscript.

Over my professional life I have taught classes on happi-

Robert Pawlicki, Ph.D.

ness in Wisconsin, Ohio and, most recently, Georgia. I wish to thank Roger Smith, an extraordinarily capable teacher and administrator of The Learning Center, a program devoted to providing intellectual nourishment to seniors in Savannah, Georgia. I am indebted to Roger for his kindness and support.

These days it is not possible to write a book that seeks a wide audience without creating a website, and I was greatly aided by Trent Kissinger who lent his creative abilities. The children who come under his teaching influence are indeed fortunate.

For the past four years I have published the essays that make up this book in the TWATL (This Week on The Landings). Because of support from publisher/editor, Jerry Sandy and Director of Production, Pam Burgess, this has been sheer pleasure. I thank them.

It was Sara Todd, a writer for the *Savannah Morning News*, who, while participating in one of my "Happiness" classes, suggested that my material was worthy of a regular column. I thank her for the recommendation that led to my column and ultimately to this book.

The TWATL column has resulted in requests for speaking engagements and the pleasure of frequent conversations in restaurants and stores. Dozens of people, who have cut out the columns to share with relatives and friends, have encouraged me and their cheerful messages helped stimulate the creation of this book.

Toward the end of my professional life as a teacher, clinician and administrator, I was the director of a chronic pain program in association with the Department of Anesthesiology at the University of Cincinnati College of Medicine. During those years of teaching and clinical work, I was exposed to the extraordinary suffering of those afflicted with chronic pain. In that setting it was possible to differentiate those who, given a chance to manage an incredibly difficult test, could absorb the life lessons necessary to meet the challenge and those who seemed unable to do so. Most of those lessons are imbedded in the essays of this book. To the many clients and patients over the years, whose identities I have always held in confidence, I give heartfelt thanks.

Robert Pawlicki, Ph.D.

Recommended Books

Books based on research data:

Ben-Shahar, T. *Happier*. McGraw-Hill Books, New York, NY, 2007.

Haidt. J. *The Happiness Hypothesis*. Basic Books, New York, NY, 2002.

Gilbert, D. *Stumbling on Happiness*, Vintage Books, New York, NY, 2005.

Lyubromirsky, S. *The How of Happiness*, The Penguin Press, New York, NY, 2008.

Myers, D. *The Pursuit of Happiness*, Avon Books, New York, NY, 1992.

Rubin, G. *The Happiness Project*, HarperCollins Publisher, New York, NY, 2009.

Seligman, M. *Learned Optimism*. Alfred A. Knopf, New York, NY, 1991.

Seligman, M. *Authentic Happiness*, Free Press, New York, NY, 2002.

Seligman, M. *Flourish*, Free Press, New York, NY, 2011.

General advice books on happiness and well being:

Kaufman, B. *Happiness Is a Choice*, Ballantine Books, New York, NY, 1991.

Hooper, J. *What Children Need to Be Happy, Confident and Successful*, Jessica Kingley, London, England, 2012.

Lama, Dalai, *The Art of Happiness*, Penguin Putnum, New York, NY, 1998.

Pawlicki, R. *Success by Another Measure*, Xlibris, Philadelphia, PA, 2002.

Prager, D. *Happiness Is a Serious Problem*, HaperCollins, New York, NY, 1998.

Weiner, E. *The Geography of Bliss*, Hachett Book Group, New York, NY, 2008.

Robert Pawlicki, Ph.D.

About the Author

Dr. Robert Pawlicki, a retired psychologist and former University professor, maintains a personal coaching practice, regularly teaches classes on happiness and other psychology topics, and writes a column entitled *Finding Happiness* for a Savannah, Georgia magazine.

In his professional career, he was director of the Behavioral Medicine Center at Drake Hospital in Cincinnati, Ohio, a multidisciplinary in-patient rehabilitation program for the treatment of chronic pain patients. Dr. Pawlicki's background includes a tenured associate professorship at the State University of New York at Oswego and the rank of full professor at both West Virginia University School of Medicine and the University of Cincinnati College of Medicine. He is the author of approximately 50 research and scholarly articles as well as the book, *Success by Another Measure: Recognizing and enhancing your character.*

Fifty Ways to Greater Well Being and Happiness

Also by Robert Pawlicki, Ph.D.

Success By Another Measure: Recognizing and enhancing your character

Readers can contact the author through his website:

www.fiftywaystogreaterwellbeingandhappiness.com